THE REFORM SCHOOL HANDBOOK
DELINQUENT
DOGS

THE REFORM SCHOOL HANDBOOK

DELINQUENT
DOGS

TONY WILKINSON

Illustrations by Kwill

Q

QUARTET BOOKS LTD

LONDON   MELBOURNE   NEW YORK

First published in 1985 by Quartet Books Ltd
A member of the Namara Group
27/29 Goodge Street
London W1P 1FD

British Library Cataloguing in Publication Data

Wilkinson, Tony
　　Delinquent dogs: the reform school handbook.
　　1. Dogs—Diseases　　2. Neuroses
　　I. Title
　　636.7'0896852　　　　　SF992.N3

ISBN 0-7043-3492-5

Designed by Namara Features Limited
Typeset by MC Typeset, Chatham, Kent
Printed and bound in Great Britain by Mackays of Chatham, Ltd, Kent

CONTENTS

Also by Tony Wilkinson
Down and Out

TONY WILKINSON

Tony Wilkinson is a reporter for BBC Television, and the presenter of "Moment of Truth", a series of personalised film documentaries first broadcast on BBC 1 in 1985.

He has written one previous book, *Down and Out* (published by Quartet). It was based on his experience of living as an outcast for four weeks on the streets of London. He slept rough with alcoholics and vagrants to find out what life was like at the bottom of the heap. His experiences were filmed secretly by the BBC and broadcast as a series by the current affairs programme "Nationwide".

He was born in Doncaster, Yorkshire in 1947, the son of a glassworker and a school teacher. After graduating from Leeds University, he worked in local newspapers, before joining the BBC in 1974.

JENNI AND HERBIE
WATSON

Jenni and Herbie Watson from Darlington, County Durham, are two of the top dog obedience competitors in Britain. In 1984, the year the Dog Reform School experiment was undertaken, Herbie Watson was the most successful competitor in the country.

They have been taking part in dog obedience competitions, on an amateur basis, for 20 years. They were selected by the BBC to run a four-day training course for problem dogs. This book records their experiences during the course and sets out the details of their training methods.

INTRODUCTION

The Reform School for Delinquent Dogs was a bold experiment. It was an attempt to take a cross-section of the toughest dogs from one big city – Manchester – and reform them through an intensive course of correction.

Using the resources of BBC Television, advertisements were placed in newspapers in and around Manchester, asking for the owners of delinquent dogs to bring their pets forward. The response was overwhelming. From every corner of the city and the countryside around, dog owners wrote in by the score, cataloguing their pets' faults. There were sad tales of dogs that ran away for days, or weeks; dogs that ganged up with others to kill cats; a dog that had ruined three suites of furniture; a dog that made amorous advances to any child under the age of seven. There were dozens of owners burdened with aggressive or anti-social pets, owners who had to apologise daily to dog-eared postmen or newspaper boys. There were dogs under court orders, dogs which stole food or clothing, and above all dog after dog which would not come when it was called.

Of the hundred or so investigated, twelve cases – the Dirty Dozen – were chosen. In each case the owner had to agree to attend the Reform School personally, since it was one

of the school's principles that the owner should be reformed along with his or her pet.

The course was run over a period of four days by two of the most successful dog obedience trainers in Britain – Jenni and Herbie Watson from Darlington, County Durham.

As this book will show, their methods worked remarkably well. Of the twelve cases, eleven ended in success. Only one dog was judged to be hopeless – a tiny psychopath called Orson.

In later chapters we show, stage by stage, how each dog was helped: how a cowardly guard-dog was taught to be brave; how a Great Dane was cured of its obsession for one woman; how a postman-biting dog was persuaded to control its blood-lust; and how several runaway dogs were brought to heel.

If you have a delinquent dog, the following pages will give you new heart. If you are thinking of owning a dog and want to prevent its becoming delinquent, this book is essential reading.

THE REFORM SCHOOL APPROACH

Most dogs are delinquent, some are allowed to become more delinquent than others. In nearly every case, canine misbehaviour is the owner's fault, and not the result of so-called "bad breeding", "personality disorder", "unhappy puppyhood" or any other excuse dog owners use to explain away their pets' crimes. You cannot keep blaming your car for every motoring accident you have, and, in the same way, sooner or later you must face the simple truth that if your dog is bad, *you* are to blame.

The Reform School approach to delinquency is to put owners and dogs in a kind of canine open prison for four days. Unlike a human borstal, we think parents must be reformed along with their wayward offspring. We regard dog owners as parents. Reform is usually harder on owners than their dogs because no one likes to admit that he or she has been an irresponsible parent. Many are hopelessly sentimental about their little delinquents and go to extraordinary lengths to avoid disciplining their dogs – for fear of losing the animal's affection.

As for the children – the delinquent dogs themselves – they are not like human adolescent offenders. Dogs never get beyond the stage of three-year-olds in their mental development. They remain in need of constant correction, attention and reassurance. If your delinquent dog is big and aggressive, it may be difficult to think of it as an eternal three-year-old child. Yet often, aggression is the result of deep insecurity. As the case histories from the Reform School show, owners who thought of their dogs as incurably vicious were astonished to find how quickly they responded to firm training methods.

In our experience, only a tiny minority of so-called "vicious" dogs are really nasty deep down. Most are only vicious because their aggression has been allowed to develop unchecked, and in some cases has been encouraged by their misguided owners. Some men actually seem to take a pride in their dog's aggression because it makes them look big. We can't think of a dafter attitude.

We feel much more sympathy with those owners who would like to control their dog's aggression but don't know how. Often, they have let their pet become boss, the leader of the pack. Dogs, after all, are pack animals. Put them in a family, and they will think of the family as their pack, in need of protection. The case of Nicky, one of the dogs on the Reform School course, was like this. She was very aggressive on her home territory, terrifying visitors to the house, and terrorising the neighbours. Yet as soon as Nicky's owners took command, she changed. Her aggression was controllable, her owners largely overcame their fear of their own pet.

Few dogs are as stupid as their owners think. Many owners are much more foolish than they would ever admit, and the most foolish assumption they make is that their dog will understand them if they shout loudly enough.

Contrary to some owners' belief, dogs do not speak English. But they do understand certain words if they are used for the same purpose time and time again. If a dog tries to bite someone, and you shout "Bad" at it every time it makes another attempt, the message will eventually get through. But many owners use different phrases every time, almost holding a conversation with their pet: "Don't do that, Rover" followed by "Leave Mrs Baxter alone", will confuse the most intelligent dog – even the one which knows who Mrs Baxter is. On the other hand, a good yank on a check-chain and a shout of "Bad", will be understood by all dogs.

In the same way, owners should always try to catch their pet in the act of criminal behaviour before punishing them. It is no use punishing a dog for tearing up your best slippers two hours after the offence has been committed. You may be angry, but punishing the dog for something so far in the past will only confuse it. As you will read, the best way to stop such behaviour is to set up a situation in which you can catch your pet in the act.

Dogs that fail to come when they are called are often the products of their

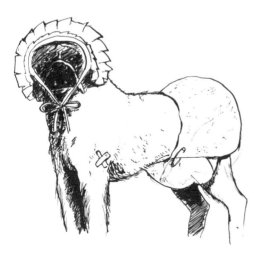

Think of him as an eternal child

owner's thoughtlessness as well. If you have taken your dog for a run in the park, and you let it off the lead, you should expect it to play as long as it likes. If you have not bothered to train it to come when it is called, how could it know any better? Many owners punish their dogs when the animal eventually decides to come. It soon gets the message that it is safer to stay away. Thus, through sheer stupidity, the owner has achieved the opposite of his or her intentions.

You must be prepared to scrap all your preconceived ideas that your dog was born vicious, or half-witted, or incapable of getting on with people in uniform. There will almost always be a reason for your dog's delinquent behaviour, and the reason in most cases is YOU. The Reform School held in the summer of 1984 is a living testament to this theory.

The advertisements were placed by BBC Television in newspapers in and around one big city – Manchester. It could have been any big city anywhere, the challenge would have been much the same. The advertisements called for the owners of delinquent dogs to come forward, to nominate their pets for intensive training at a four-day reform school. The twelve cases chosen represented a cross-section of the canine misfits from miles around. Their owners, too, had been selected for their willingness to co-operate in the experiment.

The Dirty Dozen's Casebook is an example to anyone with a problem dog. The stories provide hope for the seemingly hopeless, since eleven of the twelve cases ended in success. None of them were

Dogs do not speak English

PARLEZ-VOUS FRANCAIS?

miracle cures. All the dogs would slip back into delinquency if their owners failed to follow up the spectacular gains they made in those four days. Eleven owners left the Reform School with perfectly manageable pets, knowing that it would be their weakness or sentimentality or plain stupidity that would allow their dogs to re-offend.

Only one dog, Orson, could not be helped because in human terms he was mentally disturbed. Many of the other owners thought their dogs suffered from similar mental problems, and were quite surprised to find that they had charge of normal pets who had been largely led astray. We are confident that most of you who read the following case histories will see the similarities to your own pets.

THE REFORM SCHOOL CASEBOOK

CASE ONE

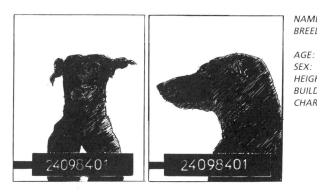

NAME: *Sam*
BREED: *Cross Labrador – German Shepherd Dog*
AGE: *Two years*
SEX: *Male*
HEIGHT: *16 inches*
BUILD: *Athletic*
CHARGE: *1) Assault on postman, occasioning actual bodily harm*
2) Theft of food from kitchen and dustbin
3) Criminal damage to a paddling pool
4) Causing hazard to motorised traffic

Sam came from a problem home. His owner, Maxine Stott, led a chaotic life, working from home as a self-employed, high-class caterer, while trying to bring up two small children, both girls, and both too young to go to school. Keeping a close eye on the dog was the last thing Maxine had time for, and over the years she had allowed him to become a dangerous pet in more ways than one.

Sam liked attacking delivery men of all kinds, dustmen, newspaper boys, anyone who came to the door without stopping to ring the bell. Sam's most prized hate figures were delivery men in uniform, especially postmen. He would lie in wait, and when they came into the drive, launch himself at them. After several attacks, most of the local postmen refused to call, and those who would still brave Sam's aggression would only make a first delivery, because in the mornings the dog was most likely to be indoors.

Sam also chased cars. When we saw him, he had been run over a few days before by his owner. This was the third time he had been involved in car accidents, the result of his love of chasing cars in the street near his home. Maxine made Sam's problems worse by failing to get him to come when she was about to go out in the car.

She told us: "It's usually when I'm in a desperate hurry, and I rush to get the children in the car, and I get the car all packed up, and I say 'Come on, Sam', and he won't come in the car, and he won't come in the house, and so we usually have this sort of battle of wits as to who gets out of the drive first, me or the dog. We end up with Sam rushing down the road after me.

"He's been knocked over three times. A couple of those were only blows, really. Once he was found unconscious by the side of the road by the police, who he immediately bit. Then once he was given a glancing blow down the drive by my sister's car, and then I finally ran over him properly."

Maxine's house, a rambling converted farmhouse with acres of garden, should be paradise for a dog, but because Sam was allowed to lead such an undisciplined life, it nearly became the death of him. Things were made worse because the family had enough money to afford several cars – all great fun to chase, and all potential killers.

Maxine said: "Sam chases my husband's car as well. It's an E-type Jaguar, and because it's a fast car, he usually gets away from him – Sam can't outpace the E-type. If I'm in the E-type, I whizz down the road and he can't catch me. It looks rather dangerous, but I can outpace him; it's quite good. My own car is not quite as fast as the E-type, and he catches me up."

From the start of the course, we regarded Maxine as a dangerous woman. Surprisingly, she quickly recognised what a liability she had been. She told us that her previous dog – like Sam, a cross-breed bought from the local dog pound – had shown many of Sam's delinquent tendencies. This dog had been so determined to attack the postman that, finding itself indoors when he called, it had launched itself through the plate-glass living-room window. The dog was badly injured, and the local postmen boycotted the house for some time.

Yet all Maxine needed was to bring consistent discipline into her dog's life for the delinquency problems to disappear. We started teaching her to make the dog sit and stay. With a lead and check-chain on, Sam was very easy to control.

It must have been quite a shock for Sam to come to terms with the new Maxine. Where she had been scatty, she was now methodical. Where she had been a soft touch, she was now strong and firm. Sam accepted the change immediately, and began to respond. This was not a fluke – all the other dogs on the course were quite prepared to adjust to the fact that their owners had undergone a personality transplant. Some of the dogs secretly hoped for a time that the old personality would come back, but once they saw no sign of wavering, they just got on with obeying the new boss in their lives.

Every time that Sam failed to sit, Maxine immediately pulled on the check-chain, sat him down with her other hand and told him he was "Bad!". Then she repeated the command to sit. Because he could not escape, Sam decided he had better get on with obeying. Within an hour, he was as good as gold. By the end of the first day, it was possible to command Sam to sit and stay. Maxine was able to drop the lead, and walk away, telling Sam to "Stay" all the time, then return to her dog, tell him she had "Finished" the exercise, and finally praise him.

We even tried getting Sam to come when he was called. Maxine ordered Sam to sit and stay, walked a short distance away, stopped, and then ordered Sam to "Come". He didn't seem too bothered about going to Maxine, but instead of doing what she normally did, trying over and over again to call the dog, this time she immediately went over to Sam, picked up his lead, and pulled him towards her shouting "Come". In the past, Maxine had tried calling the dog for a couple of hours, and by the time he came, she was so angry that she told him off. Sam must have been totally confused. In his mind, he had not been punished for staying away, yet he had been punished for coming. The opposite should have been true, and now for the first time, Maxine was rewarding him for doing the right thing.

After four days of consistent reward and punishment, Sam soon understood what was now considered right and wrong. He knew that if he failed to come when he was called, Maxine would immediately pick up his lead and pull on the check-chain, tell him he was "Bad" and repeat the command to "Come". If he obeyed, he would be told he was a "Good boy", and he would get a cuddle or even a lump of cheese.

A week after the course was over, Sam was put to the ultimate test. He was allowed off the lead in his own garden just before the postman was due to call. If the training had worked, Maxine would be able to call him away from the postman. The postman, quite nervous, arrived on his bike. Sam wanted to go into the attack, but Maxine called him . . . and he came.

No one would claim that Sam is cured. He will go back into his old ways as quickly as he came out of them if Maxine does not keep up the discipline. But she now has the means to prevent all Sam's delinquent behaviour. She can stop him chasing cars, by calling him in – and expecting him to come. For Sam, his training could prove to be a life-saver.

CASE TWO

NAME: Cleo
BREED: Bullmastiff
AGE: Three years
SEX: Female
HEIGHT: 25 inches
BUILD: Stocky
CHARGE: Assault occasioning grievous bodily harm

Cleo is big and strong and very, very vulnerable. She may look fierce, but she is afraid of the world, especially strangers' hands, umbrellas and milk floats. There is nothing that might not trigger off her nervousness, and being such a powerful dog, that makes her dangerous.

A few months before the Reform School course, Cleo had been on holiday in Wales with her owner, Bob Reade, and his family. They had called at a pub for a meal, and Bob took

Cleo for a walk in the car park. The pub landlord, who owned two boxers, took an interest in Cleo and came over. He did not know that Cleo was a nervous dog, and put his hand above her head to stroke her. Bob was holding Cleo on a lead, but he failed to spot the danger in time. The landlord was bitten so badly that one of his fingers was nearly severed. Bob was taken to court, and Cleo was sentenced to death – the sentence to be carried out if she bit anyone again.

Cleo's crime was not the result of viciousness. She bit because she was afraid. Her owner was so acutely aware of her nervousness that he had begun to communicate his fear to his pet, making the problem worse. We had to teach Bob to relax, and learn how to help Cleo cope with each new experience that might make her afraid.

We decided to tackle the worst phobias head-on, so that lesser ones would be easier to cope with. We offered her pieces of cheese, approaching her from the front so that she could see there would be no unexpected danger. Herbie spoke softly to her to make himself seem less threatening. We noticed that Bob tightened the lead as Herbie's hand came near. This acted as a warning of danger to Cleo. Bob had to be taught how to relax.

Quite soon, Cleo accepted cheese first from her owner's hand, and then, when she sensed it was safe, from Herbie's hand as well. We had given Bob the means to teach other strangers how to approach his dog safely. It might seem a tedious way of carrying on, but if the choice is having your dog put down – and Cleo was very affectionate towards Bob – or finding ways of coping, then you must be prepared to put in some effort.

We tackled umbrellas next. When they were thrust at her threateningly, she reacted far more strongly than most dogs. When they were opened suddenly, she shrank back in fear. We gave her time to inspect an umbrella at close quarters, to see it opening and shutting slowly, and then faster. Once she could see for herself that there was no real danger, she accepted the object for what it was. That is not to say, of course, that she would still not take fright if an umbrella surprised her in future, but at least Bob had a new way of helping her over her fear.

But Bob was still afraid that Cleo would bite. He told us: "She is very unpredictable, and that has made me over-cautious at times. The wife is a bit over-cautious with her too, especially when we're outside. Cleo's very good in the house with us. But if she's laid down in the house, then a stranger couldn't stroke her at all. We can stroke her now and again, but a stranger might cause her to turn round and snap."

We encouraged the other owners on the course to approach Cleo in the same way as Herbie had done, offering her tit-bits of cheese, and speaking in a soft voice to encourage her. Very gradually, Cleo tolerated this intrusion into her privacy, and by the third day, she was going up to people and accepting pieces of cheese without any fear. Everyone was still very careful not to make any sudden movements that might startle Cleo, and this seemed to work.

The milk float was Cleo's biggest fear. The Reform School arranged for a local dairy to drive one past the entire class every day. At first, Cleo was in a flat panic. At the mere sight of the milk float two hundred yards away, she began to twitch, her breathing became rapid, and she tried to pull away to safer ground. It seemed to be the sound of the bottles rattling in their crates, and the whirr of the electric motor, which frightened her as much as anything. The milk float driver, George, said he had noticed a great many dogs having the same reaction when he passed by.

The milk float stayed for an hour every day, enough time for us to familiarise Cleo with it and persuade her to overcome her fear. It would have been just as good if Bob had taken Cleo to a dairy for an hour every day. Our approach was gradual. The driver parked the milk float and sat in his cab as Bob and Herbie led the dog around it in decreasing circles. Cleo was constantly reassured that no harm would come to her, and she was not rushed into approaching too close. The driver moved the milk float forwards very slowly, and though Cleo looked apprehensive, she stayed her ground, looking up at Bob for reassurance.

When the milk float arrived on the second day, Cleo, although still anxious, allowed herself to be led straight up to the float. George, the driver, got out of his cab, and began to rearrange the empty milk bottles on the float. Herbie showed Cleo a bottle from a crate, and Cleo seemed to accept it. He picked up another bottle and quietly chinked it against the first. Again, in an atmosphere of trust, Cleo seemed to accept that there was no threat.

That night, Bob took home a milk crate filled with empty bottles so that Cleo could inspect them in the security of her own home. It seemed to work wonders. On the third day, Cleo put one paw on the milk float, then another, and finally pulled herself onto it.

Bob was amazed. We decided to ask George to take Cleo for a ride on the milk float, and Cleo seemed to love it. She sat there majestically looking down on all the other dogs as the milk float drove up and down for a good half-hour.

This was a success story, but it would be foolish to talk about a cure in Cleo's case. Bob will always have to be wary of her, and try and organise her life so that there are as few shocks and surprises as possible. A nervous dog will remain nervous all its life. The owner must decide whether the compromises he or she must make are worth the pleasure the dog can give in return.

CASE THREE

NAME:	Alice
BREED:	Great Dane
AGE:	Two years
SEX:	Female
HEIGHT:	28 inches
BUILD:	Muscular
CHARGE:	Behaviour likely to cause a breach of the peace

24098403 24098403

Alice is a dog with a mother-fixation. She would do anything at all to please the mother of the Mills household, June, and nothing to please anyone else. June was the only person who could take Alice for a walk. If the children, or anyone else tried, she would simply sit down and refuse to budge.

This sounds like a joke, but it was anything but funny for June who, as a single parent, had to find time for her job in a newspaper distribution office, and time for Alice's considerable daily exercise needs. If the children could be given the ability to take Alice for a walk, June might be given the occasional break.

June told us: "Alice is rather nervous and boisterous, and she won't entertain going out with anyone except me. If I take her out on the lead and hand her over to anyone else, she just pulls back and runs to me all the time.

"Once, I thought I would try and cure Alice. I took her out in the car with my son, and I literally dumped them a mile or so from home. I thought she would have to walk home, but after about an hour I went looking for them, and Alice was sitting in the bus shelter and wouldn't move at all with my son. He had tried to coax her, and pull her, but she just wouldn't have it."

June's two children, Harry, aged eleven, and Sara aged eight, were no match for Alice in size and strength. Alice would have to be broken of her bad habits by other people before the children could be allowed to take charge of her.

We decided that Alice would have to be introduced to the idea of walking with people other than June in a very gradual way. The first day, we attached two leads to her check-chain. The first was about two feet long. June held this, while Jenni held a four-foot lead. June and Jenni set off around the Reform School enclosure. As long as June was there, Alice was not worried by the fact that Jenni also had a lead.

After a while, Jenni asked June to drop her lead, but keep walking alongside. Alice did not protest, and we did not push her further until the second day.

The following morning, we repeated our walk with the two leads, but this time, once Alice was moving at a steady gait, Jenni told June to join the other owners. At the same time, she quickened her step, giving Alice no time to think about what had happened. She encouraged her in a confident way, and Alice seemed to sense Jenni's determination.

Jenni managed to take Alice on two complete circuits of the enclosure before she bolted back to June. It was not a pretty sight. Jenni was dragged by the lead along the wet grass until she was unable to hold on any longer. Such was Alice's determination to get back to June that she headed straight for thousands of pounds' worth of camera gear which happened to be in her direct path. It was only because June side-stepped that she altered course.

We tried again. Every time that Alice bolted back to June, she was met with June's disapproval. June pulled her check-chain, told Alice she was bad, and sent her straight back to Jenni. Later that day, June took her son Harry for a walk with Alice, and this time she was able to leave Harry in full control.

That night, June asked Harry to take Alice for a short walk while she stayed at home.

Alice did not protest. From being an apparently hopeless case of stubbornness, Alice had been transformed. It may have been the breaking down of her feelings of insecurity with people other than June, because the following day, Alice would walk with any of the other owners.

This enabled us to start training Alice in other obedience skills. Harry, although not as strong as Alice, could now get a response when he told her off. He learned how to use the check-chain with real authority, and Alice was taught to walk to heel, without pulling on the lead, how to sit and stay, and how to come when called. This was a genuine success. Alice and Harry deserved the medal we awarded them at the end of the course as top dog and trainer. It was a considerable achievement in such a short time.

CASE FOUR

```
NAME:     Nicky
BREED:    Cross Pointer
AGE:      Two years
SEX:      Female
HEIGHT:   22 inches
BUILD:    Athletic
CHARGE:   1) Assault occasioning actual
             bodily harm
          2) Threatening behaviour
```

Nicky is a classic case of a dog which considers itself boss of the house. Dogs are pack animals in the wild, and in domestic circumstances where several dogs are under the same roof, they will follow their pack instincts and develop a pecking order, a status structure. The boss dog rules the roost, and will put any challenger to his authority in its place, until the day when one of the younger dogs decides to retaliate. The winner of the battle will be the leader, and if the younger dog proves more powerful, his authority will then be accepted by the other dogs.

The odd thing about Nicky is that she was a boss dog in a household with no other dogs. She behaved in every respect as though her human companions were her pack. Her owners, Susan and Gordon Oliver were quiet, easy-going people, who tended to give in when Nicky decided to have her way. Nicky was not a vicious dog, but when we first met her, she gave every appearance of being an animal with a very vicious streak.

Susan told us: "Nicky won't let anyone near me or near the house, she just goes for them. She barks like mad, and she won't stop barking. We usually shut her away. She would bite anyone if she got near them, and she particularly hates the neighbours. When people come, I sometimes try holding her, but she'll turn her head round and go for my hand, so I suppose sometimes I do get a bit frightened of her."

Nicky bit Herbie's hand the first time they met. We had gone round to the Olivers' house, and the owners made two fundamental mistakes. The first was to allow the dog off the lead, before they were sure how she would behave. The second was that after Nicky had bitten Herbie, the Olivers tried to calm the dog down by giving her a tit-bit.

Never, never, reward a dog for bad behaviour. You are simply indulging in bribes, trying to buy good behaviour in the short-term, rather than forcing the dog to change its ways.

We got the impression that the Olivers regarded Nicky as vicious, rather than as a dominant dog which could be mastered. In fact, Nicky was doing her best, in her own eyes, to protect her pack. If she could be convinced that someone else had taken over her role, had successfully challenged her leadership, we felt Nicky would be a very different dog.

Nicky was less aggressive in the strange environment of the Reform School. Herbie approached her in a friendly way, offering his outstretched hand. Immediately, she looked as though she wanted to bite. It would have been hopeless to offer Nicky a tit-bit at this stage, as we did with Cleo (see Case Three) because, although Nicky might have accepted the gift, she would have still wanted to bite immediately afterwards.

When Herbie put his hand nearer, Nicky tried to bite, but Herbie quickly grabbed the lead and lifted Nicky off her feet. The check-chain tightened round Nicky's neck, a very unpleasant sensation for a dog. Such action may look cruel, but remember that it is only a short-term way of correcting the dog, and no permanent harm will come of it. In our opinion, it is far less cruel than letting a powerful dog which wants to taste blood have its way. Such animals do not have very rosy futures; they have to be taught as forcefully as possible that biting is not permitted.

Herbie kept his hand high on the lead, away from where Nicky could bite. He used his voice, telling her: "No, Nicky, that's very bad." Once Nicky had calmed down and realised that she was not going to be allowed to bite, Herbie managed to stroke her face, praise her for being a good girl, and then offer her a tit-bit as a reward.

With dogs like Nicky, it needs quite a forceful approach by the owner to convince their pet that they have changed. Overnight success is not possible, because the dog must be told time and again that it is not the pack leader before it accepts defeat. Nicky was, in fact, a dog capable of quite a high degree of obedience, and if her owners persevere, they could have a very likeable pet on their hands, as well as neighbours who no longer have to live in fear.

CASE FIVE

NAMES: Jack and Swivel
BREED: Cross Shih Tzu and Griffon
         Bruxellois
AGE: 18 months
SEX: Male
HEIGHT: 10 inches (Jack)
         11 inches (Swivel)
BUILD: Delicate
CHARGE: 1) Causing an affray
         2) Criminal damage to a kitchen
         door
         3) Causing a public nuisance on
         the carpet

The bible story of Cain and Abel shows how much brothers can hate each other. Jack and Swivel were very nearly as bad. They loathed each other with an intensity which was terrifying to see. Jack was the smaller of the two, and it was he who always started the fights – and always lost.

The dogs' owner, Lesley Bradshaw, had another problem to contend with as a result of the brothers' rivalry – regular messes on the floor of her home. She reckoned the dogs were well house-trained, and were vying with each other for attention, hence the puddles all over the house.

Lesley told us: "The problem is basically because there are two of them. They can't communicate with humans because they've never really needed to. For instance, house training: you find a mess on the floor so you punish them both, and one of them's thinking 'Well, I've not done anything here'. They've never really responded to me because they've never needed me to play with or anything, because they've always had each other. But now they've started fighting.

"Jack is the weaker one, and he's got a chip on his shoulder about Swivel who's always been dominant. When Jack became mature, he started cocking his leg – he was challenging Swivel to be top dog. And if Swivel was on my knee, Jack would go for him; or if Jack was nearer to me than Swivel, he'd go for Swivel. Jack always starts the fights, and Swivel always wins."

Lesley had a six-month-old baby in her house. It was obviously important to stop the dogs' fouling for reasons of hygiene. Lesley was always very careful to clean up the mess thoroughly, but it must still have been a worry to her.

We advised her to separate the two dogs, and suggested building them their own indoor kennels – not a big expense with small dogs. This would have several benefits. First, it would make sure that she knew which dog to blame for any fouling (if the problem persisted when they had their own territory); second, it would stop them fighting in her absence, and stop them being destructive – they had apparently burrowed through the kitchen door when she was out.

If the dogs had their own kennels it would be easier to give them their own toys, and something to chew when she was away. Separation would be a good idea to reduce the sense of competition that the two dogs had built up. Until the Reform School course, Lesley had left bowls of water for both dogs when she went out. This was asking for trouble. We suggested that she gave the dogs a walk and a drink outside, and then remove the drinking bowls. This would reduce the ability of the dogs to leave their scent – the habit dogs have of marking out their territory against lamp-posts and other objects. Jack and Swivel were competing with each other to leave the last trail of scent to show who was top dog, and we advised her to spray affected areas with a preparation which removes all traces of dog odour.

Jack and Swivel's problems will be long and hard to solve, while they remain together. Apart, we feel either dog would have been an excellent pet; together they will always be trouble, and prevention is the only way to make sure they behave.

CASE SIX

NAME: *Rocky*
BREED: *German Shepherd Dog*
AGE: *18 months*
SEX: *Male*
HEIGHT: *25 inches*
BUILD: *Muscular*
CHARGE: *Cowardice in the face of the enemy*

Rocky was the guard-dog who was too cowardly to guard. When intruders came to the night club premises where his owner lived, Rocky ran away and hid. When other dogs barked at him in the park, Rocky was too timid to bark back. Rocky's owner, an ex-bouncer called Phil Bieganski, was ashamed of his pet. He wanted the Reform School to make the dog brave.

Rocky had another, more delicate problem. He was car sick – so badly that it had become almost impossible for Phil to take him on even short journeys. Since Phil lived in a part of town which was some distance from any open spaces, it was important to help the dog to overcome its problems.

Jenni was not sure that Phil's requests for the Reform School to make his dog more aggressive were based on his real needs. Rocky did not live up to Phil's image of a guard-dog, and rather than try and change the dog's nature by making it ferocious, we thought it better to give the dog self-confidence, because we felt Phil would not really have liked an aggressive dog so much as a dog that could give the appearance of being aggressive when required.

Phil said: "We had Rocky when he was a pup of eight weeks old. He's very nervous with people and with other dogs. We bought him as a guard-dog for the pub and club we live in, but he doesn't seem to be doing the job that we want him to do. People knock at the door, he barks, but as soon as we open the door the dog's gone. He's very nervous like that. We tried to get people to stroke the dog, but he just won't wear it, he cowers away.

"I'd like to see Rocky be a bit more aggressive than what he is. He's got nothing, absolutely nothing. We live in a big place and it's got to be secure for my wife and kids. If we get any break-ins, the dog would just run, and they could do the business, and then go out, no problem.

"When I'm out with him, he doesn't bark once, not at people, dogs or anything. If other dogs do interfere with him, bark at him or anything, he just turns away."

We felt Rocky was not as frightened as he looked. He was immature and would grow out of his shyness if Phil could force the dog to socialise as much as possible, take him to places where there was a lot of activity, such as a local dog club where Rocky would be with other dogs and their owners. The Reform School was just that sort of environment, and Rocky responded quickly when he realised that no one was going to harm him.

But first, we had to enable Rocky to travel the five miles to the Reform School without being car sick. Jenni had read a medical article which described how young children had been cured of car sickness by layers of newspapers placed on the car seats. The newspaper acted as an electrical earth, cutting down the amount of static electricity in the car.

Phil put newspapers down on the seats and floor of his car, and Rocky improved immediately. There was a slight queasiness the first trip, but by the second and third, he was perfectly happy to travel in the car. Phil was delighted.

Next, we tried to teach Rocky to bark on command. This was hard, because Rocky did not seem aware that he had a voice. We decided to force him to speak to Phil, by tying the dog up, and then having his owner call him from a distance. The sheer frustration of wanting to go to his owner, while being prevented from doing so, would leave Rocky with only one way of communicating – by barking.

The theory was simple. Every day for up to half an hour at a time, we put Rocky to the test, holding him on his lead while Phil called him from a distance. Three days later, Rocky had managed only the smallest whimper. Jenni kept encouraging him by pointing at Phil and telling him to "Speak!". But Rocky would not speak.

Then we noticed that Rocky had taken a fancy to a Jack Russell Terrier called Lucy. Lucy was quite a girl, as all the other dogs on the course noticed. Phil picked Lucy up in his arms and ran off with her. It took another ten minutes of sheer torture, before Rocky finally caught on. He barked, he responded to the praise, and he barked again. Success. But Rocky would need much more socialising before he would bark on command.

In fact, Rocky was so responsive to the rest of the training at the Reform School that we considered him ideal material for obedience competitions. Phil was so proud of his dog by the end of the course that he was seriously thinking of taking the suggestion up. Rocky might never be the guard-dog that Phil had wanted, but he would be a wonderful pet – and with a bit of luck, a dog that could pretend to be ferocious when the need arose.

CASE SEVEN

NAME:	Blackie
BREED:	Whippet
AGE:	Three years
SEX:	Male
HEIGHT:	18 inches
BUILD:	Slim
CHARGE:	1) Assault occasioning actual bodily harm
	2) Causing an affray on the race track

Blackie is a dog trained to race after an artificial hare. Like other racing dogs, he has been bred to chase and kill. Blackie's problem was that he didn't know how to control his aggressive instincts. He bit other dogs on the track, and he bit other people who came near his home.

Blackie's owner, Christine MacLean told us: "He chases the postman, the milkman, anybody who comes up the path. If he can catch them, he'll have a nibble at them. He jumps over the garden wall and fence all the time, and he barks at anything going past – bicycles, children. He just thinks he owns the whole road.

"On the race track, he's very fast. If he didn't fight so much he'd win races, but he doesn't win because he's aggressive, and even with a muzzle on, he still fights."

This is a difficult case, because Blackie is expected to be both a racing dog and a pet. Whippets do not, by and large, make good pets, but when they are given two contradictory roles to play, their behaviour at home is likely to get worse.

We felt that while Blackie continued to race, the problems at home would continue. Since everything had been tried to stop her fighting on the race track, without success, it was probably a good idea to abandon any thought of a racing career, and concentrate on Blackie's behaviour at home.

We decided to teach Chris basic control of her dog, so that she could prevent attacks happening. If she could get the dog to come when he was called, she would stand a chance of bringing him back when he bolted out of the door. If she could control the dog on a lead when she was out walking, make sure that he walked to heel, and would sit and stay on command, then she could stop him attacking dogs that came within striking distance – provided she kept alert, and stopped the aggression before it developed.

After a few days, Blackie became a lot more obedient, and much more of a pleasure for Chris to own. He started to come when he was called – not in all circumstances, but in most. In an atmosphere of discipline, Blackie seemed less aggressive than he had been in the past.

Chris will have to be very strict, and very careful in the future. The dog will have to be much more restricted than most pets. Chris will have to stop Blackie getting out into the garden where he could get over the wall. Most of the time the dog will have to be kept indoors, and with children going in and out, Chris will have to secure the dog in one room and tell the children not to go in that room without permission.

Outside the home, Chris must never let Blackie off the lead, except when exercising the dog. Even then, she must choose times of day when there are no other dogs around – unless she can be sure Blackie will come when he is called. She must always call the dog before trouble starts. If she does not, Blackie will almost certainly slip back into his old ways.

CASE EIGHT

NAME:	Lucy
BREED:	Jack Russell Terrier
AGE:	18 months
SEX:	Female
HEIGHT:	13 inches
BUILD:	Voluptuous
CHARGE:	1) Going absent without leave
	2) Criminal damage to visitors' clothing

Lucy is a girl who can't say no. To be strictly truthful, she does not want to say no. Lucy wants to be loved twenty-four hours a day, by as many people and as many other dogs as possible.

Lucy's problem is that she doesn't know when to stop. She smothers visitors to the house with affection, she goes flat out to attract the attention of not just one or two dogs in the park, but all the dogs in the park, and when Lucy is off the lead, there is no stopping her – and no calling her back.

Her owner, Jennifer Barlow told us: "The worst problem is that you can't get her back. If you let her out in the park, or she gets out of the garden, which she does with amazing skill whenever she can, she just shoots off into the distance, and you have to spend about two hours running round trying to round her up.

"The other problem with her is jumping up at people when they come to the house. She dives all over them, jumps up and down at them, goes crazy. She's very lovable, she jumps all over everybody because she loves everybody and anybody. The visitors go away nearly in shreds. If anybody's got tights on, they go away with them full of ladders and covered in mud or anything."

Lucy got a nickname at the Reform School – Juicy Lucy. Although she was spayed, she had the most amazing ability to make herself attractive to all the other dogs. Given the opportunity, they would chase her round and round the enclosure, until Lucy decided she wanted to be caught. She would accept their attentions for a short time, and then she would be off again.

We decided that Lucy needed a stringent course in recall – coming when called. This was made easier by her fondness for cheese. First, we taught her how to sit and stay. She was so keen on Jennifer's praise, and the reward of cheese, that at the end of the first day, she was sitting and staying on command. When Jennifer walked in front of her holding the lead, repeating the command "Stay", Lucy did not waver. By the end of the second day, Jennifer was able to remove the lead and walk about ten feet away from Lucy.

We went on to the second stage. Instead of returning to her dog, praising her and rewarding her with cheese, this time Jennifer asked Lucy to come to her. She told Lucy to sit and stay, walked about ten feet away, repeating the command to stay, and then she told Lucy to "Come". Lucy flew towards Jennifer, obeyed the command to sit, and then waited patiently for her reward of cheese and Jennifer's praise.

By the third day, Lucy was so advanced that we took her, with a couple of the other dogs, outside the enclosure to train her to come even when other pleasures beckoned her away. We attached a thirty-six-foot rope to each dog's collar, and let them run and play. The dogs were aware they were attached to a line, but also aware that they had considerable freedom of movement.

Then the owners started to tell their dogs to come. Jennifer let Lucy go a foot away at first, then called her back, told her to sit, and gave her praise and a reward of cheese. Gradually the distance was extended, until Lucy was playing with the other dogs at the end of the rope, and coming as soon as Jennifer called.

Finally, we took the dogs off the lead, and tempted Lucy into a chase. She could not resist. For two or three minutes, Lucy hared round in front of the other dogs – Sam and Patch – loving every minute of it. When Jennifer called her, she looked at Sam, saw that he was still willing to chase, and ignored Jennifer's call.

It was vital that Jennifer should not go to Lucy, because that would have started another chase, this time between owner and dog. Instead, she gave the dog a verbal ticking off, telling her she was "Bad". We reinforced the ticking off, and Lucy became very much aware that she had done something wrong. Jennifer called her again, in a tone of voice that was friendly but firm, and this time, Lucy responded. It is useful to have someone else with you at times like this, because they can reinforce your disapproval, while the owner can seem firm and friendly – the sort of owner who will give you a reward if you decide to stop being disobedient.

By the end of the fourth day, Lucy seemed to look forward to Jennifer's voice calling firmly "Lucy, come!". In front of the whole class, she sat while her owner walked a full one hundred yards, turned and called. We could see that Lucy was very interested in something other than her owner. Unseen by us, Jennifer's mum had arrived. Yet as soon as the command was given, Lucy obeyed Jennifer. Lucy had learned to control her need for another person's attention, in this case Jennifer's mum. She now knew that she got even more praise if she obeyed first, and showed affection second.

CASE NINE

NAME:	Paddy
BREED:	Old English Sheepdog
AGE:	20 months
SEX:	Male
HEIGHT:	24 inches
BUILD:	Stocky
CHARGE:	1) Common assault
	2) Criminal damage to visitors' clothing
	3) Theft of golf balls

Paddy is the dog the Dulux paint company should use to advertise off-white paint. He looked a big softie, but after nearly two years of being allowed to get his own way, he was a spoiled brat who could be a thorough nuisance.

He was one of the most obstinately disobedient dogs on the Reform School course, partly because his owner, Janie Easthope, had always given in to him. This is what she told us:

"The main problem is his strength and my weakness. He is so big; he is six stone and very strong and very, very fit, and he tells me where he's going.

"I take him for walks on the golf course, and he will not come when I call him. Some days he can be really, really good. If there's nobody there, he's excellent, and he will come back. But if he sees anything else more interesting, he'll be off. We now must have about three hundred golf balls which he's managed to find by foul means and other sorts.

"The main problem in the home is that he tries to jump up all the time, he's just too exuberant. When people come to the house, the doorbell goes, and you're lucky if you beat him to the door. If Paddy gets there first, you spend half an hour wrestling with him, trying to get to the door knob. If that's not frightened the people away, he leaps all over them, and that finally finishes them off."

Paddy could hurt people. He was not a dog who liked biting, but he used craft to get people into a position where he could catch them off guard and butt them with the top of his head. All the time, he looked the picture of good-natured innocence.

It was hard work teaching him to obey. He tried to bite Herbie's hand when he realised that a command to sit was really meant. At this stage, it took a fair amount of physical strength to master Paddy – something that Janie would not have been able to do alone. That is not to say that Janie could not have taught Paddy basic obedience at an earlier stage, before he was too big.

Janie found it hard to see the dog she regarded as her baby suddenly being told he was bad. She was not going to have her dog smacked for being naughty. Of course, we did not do anything vicious or cruel, we were just firm with the dog. But after a few days, her attitude slowly began to change. Paddy responded to firmness, and began to sit and stay on command.

We put him on a long lead. We would let him wander off to find something interesting, and then Janie would call him. At first he was very resistant to her call. Herbie gave a hard tug on the check-chain, and Janie told Paddy he was bad. The next time she called "Paddy, come", the slightest hesitation was punished by a pull on the check-chain. This time, he came and Janie praised him. All was forgiven, and Paddy wandered off again. It took a great deal of punishment and reward to break through Paddy's stubborn disobedience, but by the end of the fourth day, we let him run without a lead and Janie managed to call him back – most of the time.

Paddy's problem was as much to do with Janie's attitude towards her pet, as anything. She had bought a stubborn dog and made him more stubborn by letting him have his own way. At the end of the course, it was plain that Janie would have to keep up her new firmness for several months to achieve really consistent results.

As for the three hundred golf balls that Paddy had stolen, we advised Janie to take them back to the golf club and sell them. It would be tactful not to take the thief along with her when she did so.

CASE TEN

NAME:	*Patch*
BREED:	*Springer Spaniel*
AGE:	*Four years*
SEX:	*Female*
HEIGHT:	*19 inches*
BUILD:	*Average*
CHARGE:	*1) Theft of food from kitchen*
	2) Going absent without leave
	3) Conduct likely to cause a breach of the peace

Patch's owner, Morag Antrobus, probably needed more training than her wayward dog. She simply could not bring herself to punish Patch for doing something wrong. Morag blamed it on Patch's big brown soulful eyes. The dog could have got away with murder. In the meantime, she got away with just about everything else.

Morag told us: "Patch is just an extremely boisterous dog. She's neurotic, she jumps, she bounces, she barks, she steals, she runs away, she chews, she won't walk to heel, she won't come back when she's called. If you can think of anything that a dog shouldn't do, Patch does it.

"I get a very sore throat from shouting at her. There comes a point when the dog seems to be stronger than me. I admit that I am at fault, but I can't always control her because I give in. It's easier to give in than it is to continue to try and make her do what I want.

"She's got such soulful eyes, you see. I go to smack her, and she rolls over onto her stomach, so you can't smack her, because you're not going to attack her stomach, are you? So, she rolls over, shakes her legs in the air, looks at you with these great big brown eyes, and I laugh."

Even if Morag had been stronger-willed, she would have had a problem in controlling Patch, because the dog had an entirely unsuitable lead. Morag had bought a strong, chain-link lead which slipped through her hands when the dog pulled away. Her hands had become very sore. The check-chain, too, was made of thick metal links which snagged when pulled tight, and failed to let the chain close round the dog's neck.

We replaced the chain-link lead with one made of strong, fine-quality leather. The check-chain was replaced by one made of fine links – just as strong, but with a much smoother action. Both were vital to bring Patch under control, especially since with other dogs, she showed quite an aggressive streak, snapping at their heels. Morag needed to be able to prevent her dog getting into trouble.

Patch was hyper-active. She was always on the move, always making a noise, an annoying combination of bark and whimper which threatened to disrupt the class. Jenni had to tell her: "No, Patch, bad girl. Now quiet!". When she stopped barking, Jenni immediately praised her, telling her how clever she was. Morag then took over. She knew the tone of voice that would get respect, and the words to use. It was the start of Patch's reform.

Patch's progress came quickly, despite her stubborn, attention-seeking temperament. Within a few days, Patch was walking to heel very well. Morag had to keep using the check-chain to enforce discipline. It was hard work persuading Patch to sit at first, but the dog responded to rewards of cheese, especially when Morag was teaching her to come when called.

There were still attempts by Patch to pull ahead when walking to heel, but Morag reacted very quickly with a firm pull on the check-chain, and the words: "No, Patch, that's bad." This constant correction took a great deal of effort on Morag's part, because Patch's faults were so many. No sooner had she got Patch to sit correctly, than the dog would start to whimper, needing more correction.

As for Patch's aggression to other dogs, she met her match when she took on Alice, an eight-stone Great Dane. Patch ended up with quite a sore flank where Alice's teeth sank in. Yet this side of Patch's nature will be difficult to correct. To prevent incidents happening Morag must keep up her efforts to control her dog. In Patch's case, it will be a long struggle.

CASE ELEVEN

NAME:	Snowy
BREED:	Greyhound
AGE:	Three years
SEX:	Female
HEIGHT:	27 inches
BUILD:	Slim
CHARGE:	1) Causing a public nuisance on the carpet
	2) Failure to obey orders

Snowy was a dirty dog, an apparently stupid dog, a dog with a huge inferiority complex. Most of that changed in the four days she was on the Reform School course. She ended up a clean dog, a dog who suddenly understood what her owner wanted from her, and a dog who had really begun to enjoy life for the first time.

Snowy lived in the same house as another delinquent on the course, Blackie the Whippet. Because Blackie was such a dominant, aggressive dog, Snowy's natural tendency to shyness was made worse. Her owner, Chris MacLean told us: "She's been a kennel dog for two years, so she's not house-trained, and when we first got her, she'd never been in a house, so everything was completely new to her. She can walk on a lead, but other than that, she doesn't know any basic commands.

"She's permanently frightened. When you call her to come, she's very, very timid. She isn't an intelligent animal at all; I tell her to come and she goes. She thinks she's the same size as the other dogs, so she tries to get out through the same spaces, and she jumps through plate glass windows when she doesn't make it.

"She walks all over dogs and cats that are smaller than her, but she doesn't mean to, she just doesn't know she's done it."

The first priority for Snowy was to solve her toileting problems. Chris had been in the habit of feeding Snowy one large meal a day. We asked her to change to three small meals a day. Straight away, there was an improvement. Snowy was clean for two nights out of the first three.

Snowy had not really understood her place in the home, and she certainly had not understood what Chris had been asking her when commands were given. "She doesn't even know how to sit," Chris told us. She was right. It took two days of pushing and praising before Snowy suddenly caught on. From then on, it was a party piece that Snowy would proudly demonstrate to anyone who cared to watch. In fact, she began to sit so much, that after three days, the fine covering of hair on her rump had worn away, and we had to apply antiseptic cream to soothe the soreness. This was the first case of nappy rash we had seen in a dog, and it demonstrated how willing Snowy was to please, once she knew what was wanted.

Within a couple of days, Snowy was really enjoying the obedience training, looking up at Chris, appreciating the attention she was getting. Snowy also had the self-confidence to be naughty every now and then, especially when she was off the lead. She would come when called most times towards the end of the course, but once in a while, she would take off at a gallop, to show all the other dogs how fast she could run. Chris showed she could bring the situation under control by telling Snowy she was bad, and calling her again. When Snowy came, she was praised, and it was obvious how much she liked her owner's approval.

Greyhounds do not make the best pets because they have been bred for centuries for one purpose – to chase and kill game. Yet Snowy showed all the signs of a dog which could respond to command, and show affection. With patience, Chris could even solve her house-training problems by teaching her pet to relieve herself in one allotted place in the garden. That would be success indeed.

CASE TWELVE

NAME:	Orson
BREED:	Cross Cairn Terrier
AGE:	Three years
SEX:	Male
HEIGHT:	Nine inches
BUILD:	Light
CHARGE:	Assault occasioning grievous bodily harm

Orson may be small, but he is deadly. He was the only dog to succeed in biting not only Herbie, other dogs at the Reform School, but his owner as well. In 20 years of working with hundreds of dogs, this is only the second case where we felt a dog's temperament could not be changed enough to make it into an acceptable pet. Orson could not be cured, and we recommended that he should be humanely killed.

Orson's owner, Stanley Hall, is a big man – six feet one inch tall and 13 stones in weight. He owned a Dobermann Pinscher before Orson, and found it very much easier to handle.

Orson was found abandoned by the roadside when he was a puppy. Stanley and his wife took him home and bottle-fed him, saving the dog's life. But he returned their love with bad temper and aggression, biting them whenever he could. Since then, their life has become a misery, and by the time Stanley took him to the Reform School, he was ready to have the dog put down.

He told us: "Orson bites anybody and anything. It's his unpredictability that's the worst thing. He's a perfect angel one minute, and then the next minute you've got two lumps out of your hand.

"In the street, he's always on a lead. Anyone who comes near is a problem. You've got to turn round straight away and say 'Don't touch him'. On one occasion, I tied him up outside a supermarket when I was going shopping. An old dear of about 70 walked up and I immediately said: 'Don't go near him, love, he bites'. She said: 'Oh, he won't bite me', and she bent down to stroke him. Well, he literally launched himself at her, and she nearly had a cardiac arrest on the spot."

On the first day of the course, Herbie introduced himself to Orson very gently. The dog had no hesitation in biting his hand rather badly. The bleeding did not stop for several hours. Orson also tried to bite every other dog that came near him, and succeeded several times. Stanley could do little but drag him away.

We decided to try teaching Orson basic obedience. This time, when he became aggressive with Herbie, he was hung up by his choke-chain for a few seconds as punishment. But Orson would not stop his aggression. It took quite severe punishment to make him calm down at all. This was not teaching so much as Herbie's domination of the dog by physical superiority.

As the course progressed, it became obvious that Orson was susceptible to certain kinds of training. He would walk to heel well, and would sit and stay on command. But he remained aggressive as soon as he was given the opportunity. If he was walking to heel and he passed close by a dog he did not like, he would try to bite that dog. It was as if he had two personalities. The truth was that Orson quite liked the praise that came when he performed to order, but when something he liked better came along such as the opportunity to bite someone or some other dog, he continued to do as he liked, forgot about the obedience class and reverted to his usual aggressive self.

Stanley told me that his wife had been bitten badly while the couple were on the beach during a holiday weekend.

"We were on the dunes," he said, "*Sunday Times, News of the World*, a nice cup of coffee and . . . peace. Orson was under the wife's chair having a snooze. Then all of a sudden, her foot upset him and . . . clunk! A hole in the foot . . . he had a lump out of it. He nearly got put down then. The decision was nearly made, but it was a Bank Holiday weekend, and of course you can't get hold of a vet, and by the time the Tuesday morning had come, he'd been reprieved."

By the end of the course, Orson had not improved. Stanley's wife told us that she lived in terror of the dog. Sometimes, she had been trapped for hours in her own home, afraid to move the dog from her lap in case it turned on her. Only Stanley ever succeeded in picking the dog up, but on the third day of the course he too was bitten. He was trying to stop Orson biting someone else at the time.

This may seen comical, but no one in Stanley's family was laughing. His first grandchild had just been born, and he had to face up to the danger a vicious dog can pose to a baby. Once the child begins to crawl Orson might bite it on the face, scarring it for life. It is a risk we advised Stanley not to take. His dog was in human terms a psychopath, a creature which showed no sign of remorse after each attack. The only sensible course was to have Orson put down. The alternative was a life so restricted, it would not be worth contemplating.

THE DELINQUENCY FILE

If you have read all the stories from the Reform School casebook, it will be pretty obvious by now that certain problems occur again and again. Few dogs have only one delinquent tendency. Most have a whole cluster, often because their owners have made several mistakes rather than just one.

In the following pages, we set out the main problems, one by one, and show you how the Reform School tackles them. Surprisingly, simple obedience training in the basic commands works wonders with most dogs. Many owners think they have mastered these anyway, and that their dog's problem lies elsewhere. But in case after case, the owner who claims to be able to get his dog to sit and stay has only really managed the feat on the dog's good days, the days when it chooses to be obedient. Consistency is the key. You must be able to get your pet to obey when it does not feel like obeying.

There is no room for sentimentality. You must master your dog for its own good. It may sound contradictory, but an obedient dog is usually happier than a disobedient one, because it knows its place in the world. Some owners cannot bring themselves to speak harshly to their dogs or use the check-chain sharply enough. This is because they have made the fundamental mistake of confusing discipline with punishment. All obedience training should be done with love. For every firm call of "Bad", there should be five or six calls of "Good boy" when the dog even partly succeeds in following your command.

Soon, your pet will begin to understand that there are endless rewards for doing things right, and not much point in doing them wrong. You achieve this by patience – letting the dog know that you will repeat an exercise time and time again until he gets it right. This is far more effective than the counter-productive short cut of doling out punishment in equal measure to praise.

Look through each section problem by problem, see which apply to your dog, and then read how to solve your problems.

AGGRESSIVE DOGS

Dogs are aggressive for different reasons. It is foolish to lump all aggressive dogs together, because their problems have such varied causes, and need very different kinds of treatment. We shall deal with the problems and the cures one by one. You must decide which category your dog fits.

1) THE BOSSY VARIETY

A dog is naturally a pack animal. Its behaviour is largely determined by its instinct to be led by another member of the pack, or to become leader itself. Coupled with that is every dog's desire to protect its territory and its family. When you own a pet, you are regarded by it as its family. Dogs bark when strangers approach your house because their instinct tells them to repel invaders who may do the family some harm. It is the combination of these two instincts, the desire to compete with other dogs for leadership, and the wish to defend home territory, that can result in unwanted aggression in your dog.

As we saw in the last chapter, one of the dogs on the Reform School course, Nicky, fitted this category. She regarded herself as the pack leader in her family, and she protected the house by barking and growling at strangers, and biting them if she was allowed anywhere near.

Nicky did not stop her aggressive behaviour once strangers had been welcomed into the house by her owners; she continued to bark and bite. She did not respond to orders to be quiet, and could only be controlled by being restrained on a lead. This is typical of a dominant dog. Nicky saw herself as boss of the household, and *she* decided who was welcome and who was not – not her owners.

Such dogs can be controlled if an owner decides to take over the role of being pack leader. This means first of all recognising that you have allowed the dog to set the agenda, allowed it to become boss. Once you have admitted your weakness, you are half way to solving your problem.

When you have decided to become the boss, you must prove to the dog that you

Take over as pack leader

have changed. Set up a situation you can control. If, like Nicky, your dog tries to attack visitors to the house, arrange for a person the dog dislikes to call. Make sure the dog is on its lead just before the visit, and fit a check-chain so that you can punish it for misbehaviour.

You will need two people inside the house to make training effective – one to answer the door, and you to restrain the dog. As soon as the visitor knocks, you must take hold of the dog's lead. Let him bark until the door has been answered – after all there may be times when you want him to have this response. As soon as the visitor has been welcomed into the house, you must order your dog to keep quiet. Use a key-word such as "Quiet", say it loudly and firmly, and if the dog continues to bark and snarl, give the dog a good strong yank on the check-chain.

When you correct the dog you should tell him he is "Bad". Link this with the command "Quiet" until the dog stops

barking. It may take ten or twenty repetitions before he responds. The longer you have let him get away with it in the past, the harder it will be.

If he tries to bite you, use the check-chain to prevent him. By holding it high above his head, your hand is away from his mouth and his teeth cannot reach you. You must overcome any fear of your pet, and really boss him. Half-hearted attempts at making him be quiet are worse than useless because they will only let the dog know that nothing has changed, and that he is still pack leader.

Whatever happens, do not stop your discipline until you get the desired response. As soon as the dog is quiet, tell him he is a "Good boy", and reward him with something he likes, such as a small piece of cheese.

When you have repeated this training over several days, place a small bowl of cheese near the front door so that every visitor can give some to the dog. This will soon make the dog associate visitors with a reward – a reward that is only earned if he stops his aggression towards them. You will have given your guests a passport into the dog's good books.

It will take days, even weeks before the dog finally gets the message that things have changed for good. Many people find it hard to believe that dogs will accept the changes in you, especially if you feel that you are still as soft, deep down, as you always were. But you can be two people, a strict person with the dog, and your usual self with the rest of the family. You must teach the other members of the family to behave to the dog in the same way. Beware of those weaker members of the family who want you to give up so that they can have an easier life in the short-term. That way leads to disaster. The dog will realise that you have tried to dominate him and failed. He will be back as boss, his leadership reinforced.

The technique we have described for controlling aggression in dogs towards visitors to the house can be applied to any other circumstances where the dog displays aggression. If he is aggressive to people in the street, set up a street encounter so that you have the time to discipline him properly. If he is aggressive to other dogs in the park, make sure you have allowed enough time to punish him again and again until he stops. Of course, by punishment, we do not mean that you should hit your dog. The use of the check-chain, and the word "Bad" should be enough. And never forget to praise the dog when it eventually gets things right. You can never overdo this – give the dog a stroke and cuddle as well, and it will obey faster next time.

This is how to use the check-chain. It

should be made of fine-link steel, and should slip freely on the left hand side of the dog's neck. This is so that when you walk with the dog by your left leg, as you should always do, the chain does not hurt the animal by snagging against the links (see diagram).

Mostly, the check-chain will be used as a gentle control, a warning that it could be tightened further if bad behaviour persists. The use of a really sharp pull should be reserved for downright disobedience. For example, if you have ordered your dog to walk to heel (an important discipline if he is aggressive towards other people in the street), you should start by commanding the dog, using a key-word, "Heel". If you have never trained him to do this before, he will not understand the key-word, and will almost certainly continue either to pull on the lead, or lag behind.

You should use the check-chain gently at first to pull the dog into the correct position by your left leg. As you do this, you should command him with the word "Heel". If you have chosen a spot where there are few distractions for your dog, he should walk close beside you for a short distance. If he does, praise him by telling him he is a "Good boy". If he then pulls on his lead, you must give a good yank on the check-chain to correct his disobedience. You must reinforce this by the word "Bad", so that he is left in no doubt about your feelings.

At first, he will not understand what you want him to do. You must show him by pulling the check-chain tight and guiding him close to your left leg. As soon as he walks a few paces in this position, tell him he is a "Good boy". As soon as he starts to move out of position tighten the check-chain a little, repeating the command "Heel". Reward him for the slightest sign of obedience by telling him he is a "Good

boy", and when he starts to pull away repeat the command "Heel". When he completely disobeys, yank the check-chain and tell him he is "Bad".

Many owners are not tough enough with aggressive dogs, because they are nervous about being bitten. It may be that you should ask someone less nervous to help with your training. Once the dog has recovered from the initial shock of being given a firm pull on the check-chain, and once he realises that he cannot bite your friend's hand (provided of course your friend holds the check-chain high enough above the dog's neck), then after an hour or so, you can take over and continue with the same obedience lesson.

Even if your dog is aggressive in only one situation, it is a good idea to train him in basic obedience. A dog that will sit and stay, for example, is far easier to keep out of trouble than a dog which has not been trained to do so. Obedience training will give you the means to avoid trouble.

Above all, bossy dogs must be put in their place all the time. You should put such dogs to the test over trivial things, and master them. If you are taking such a dog into a room, you should insist on walking in first. If the dog does not like it, discipline him in the ways we have described and praise him when he obeys. Occasionally you should take his feeding dish away for short periods during mealtimes, to show that he cannot have his own way all the time. Only by dominating the dog will you force it to be less aggressive. If you really try, you should succeed within a few weeks. If after then, the dog is still not cured, it may be that the problem is worse than you first thought. It could be one of the other two categories of aggressive dog, or, if the dog is male, you may have to resort to castration.

2) THE NERVOUS VARIETY

Dogs which are aggressive through fear are a very much bigger problem. There are some dogs which are afraid of the world, some which have specific anxieties. Both kinds can be trained out of their fears, up to a point. But you will never take away the dog's deep-seated problems, all you can do is help the animal to live with them.

Taking part in the Reform School training were several nervous dogs. Cleo, a powerful Bullmastiff, was the most difficult. She was not aggressive in any real sense. She was so terrified of the world that her aggression was really defensive. Unfortunately, because she was so strong, she could do a great deal of damage. On the one occasion when her owner dropped his guard, Cleo bit the hand of a stranger who had tried to stroke her. He ended up in hospital, and Cleo ended up in court. She was sentenced to death, the sentence to be carried out if she bit anyone again. Yet although Cleo seemed like an aggressive dog, her action had been the result of fear.

All you can do in cases like Cleo's is to make their world into a less terrifying place. You already know what frightens them most; what you must do is to show them stage by stage, that things are not really as bad as they seem.

Let us say your dog is frightened of the noise your vacuum cleaner makes. It is a good idea to show the dog the vacuum cleaner when it is switched off. Put the dog on a lead, and get someone else to switch the machine on briefly. If the dog is frightened, calm him down, switch off the machine, and lead him towards it. Keep reassuring him. Lead him away to a safe distance, and again switch the machine on briefly. Repeat the process again and again, so that the dog knows the machine will do him no harm. Once the dog seems to accept that he is safe, take him into another room, and have your friend switch on the vacuum cleaner out of sight. The dog may again be frightened. Keep the machine turned on, and lead the dog back to it, so that he can see where the noise is coming from. Switch the machine off, and let the dog see that it is harmless. Take your time, and keep giving reassurance.

There are no short cuts with nervous dogs. You must simply take each frightening object or noise, and patiently show the dog that it is harmless. It may take a week for you to succeed in making his world less frightening in only one way. But every success means that your life is less restricted, and that your dog is more of a pleasure to own.

Some dogs are nervous of people, and show their fear, like Cleo, through aggression. It may be that after a few nasty experiences, you have decided to steer clear of crowds, or anywhere you might meet strangers. This is sensible. But it is possible to make your dog more sociable, and less of a danger.

If you set up circumstances where the dog can be introduced to two or three strangers – friends you have warned – you can get him used to company in a gentle way. Your friends should not be nervous types themselves, and they should be given pieces of cheese to offer the dog. Once a dog will take food from a stranger's hand, he is half way to accepting strangers stroking him (strictly under your supervision, of course).

After a few weeks you can start to teach the dog basic obedience, in the presence of your friends. This will give the dog something to occupy his mind. Keep him on the lead all the time to prevent any acts of aggression. Every time your dog achieves success in sitting and staying on the lead, or in walking to heel, reward him with a piece of cheese. Then get one of your friends to reward him with an extra piece of cheese. It may take several attempts before the dog does not react aggressively to the stranger's offer of cheese. Take your time; old habits die hard. Encourage your friends to join in your praise of the dog, so that he can see that they are not a threat.

Eventually it may be possible to invite strangers into your home in the same way as we outlined for dominant dogs. They should be given tit-bits for the dog at the door, and instructed to adopt a friendly tone of voice. The dog, meanwhile, should be held on a lead in a back room. Any signs of aggression should be dealt with severely. The visitor should be introduced into the room at a distance from the dog. Again there should be punishment for any misbehaviour by use of the check-chain and the key-word "Bad". As soon as the dog obeys, praise him and reward him with a tit-bit. Continue the obedience lesson, and gradually let your visitor come nearer.

It may take a few minutes of this kind of breaking the ice every time a visitor calls. But it is better that you do this, than have the dog locked up all the time, barking nervously out of sight.

As you will have read, Cleo was one of the success stories at the Reform School. She managed to overcome her fear of milk floats, after a lot of gentle persuasion. She realised that they would do her no harm. She would accept tit-bits from the other owners, provided they approached her in the right way. But Cleo will always be a nervous dog, and her owner must be on his guard all the time; showing visitors to the home how to behave towards her; carefully stage-managing any trips into the outside world.

If you are prepared to limit your life in these ways, to place restrictions on what you can and cannot do, you may decide that it is worth persevering with a nervous dog. If you are not, it may be cruel to the dog to let it live. Life for some nervous dogs can be hell, because they are not in control of their circumstances – they do not know when the next frightening object or noise, or person may be coming along, and some owners end by taking the easy option and locking their pet away. It is up to you to decide, but if your nervously aggressive dog does not respond to your patient persuasion after several months of trying, consider taking it to the vet to be put down.

3) THE PLAIN NASTY VARIETY

We have to face the fact that some dogs are plain nasty. There are, thank goodness, not many of them around. We have met only two in our 20 years' experience of dog training. One, as you have read, was on the Reform School course – Orson. (See Chapter 2.)

Many people mistake dominant dogs for those with psychopathic tendencies. The difference is that dominant dogs will usually respond to firm training and obey the command to stay, when they feel like biting. With plain nasty dogs, their desire to hurt will always overcome their desire to please their owner.

Again this is a judgement only you can make. You must have really tried to get your dog to respond for several months before you reach any conclusions about which of our three categories he falls into. It would be tragic if you wrote off your dog as being plain nasty when the fault is really yours for failing to train him properly.

In Orson's case, Stanley had really tried to make his dog obey, and Orson came out as one of the dogs near the top of the class for some obedience exercises. But put temptation in his way in the form of a passing ankle or another dog, and he would almost invariably succumb. Orson bit Stanley's wife with no provocation whatsoever when they were sitting on a beach. With nervous dogs, or with dominant dogs, there is always a reason for their aggression – whether it is fear or the defence of territory – with plain nasty dogs there is often no provocation for their behaviour.

In the end, you must take responsibility for your dog's actions. If, after really trying, its viciousness remains uncontrolled and unpredictable, you must seriously think about a visit to the vet to have the animal put down. But you must really try everything first to make sure that the dog is the problem and not your laziness or your weakness.

DIRTY DOGS

Dirty dogs have gone far beyond the first stages of house training (see Chapter 4). They are dogs who have learned bad habits and must be corrected as soon as possible.

In nearly all cases, dogs are dirty because their owners let them get into bad ways. A typical example is the lazy owner who decides that instead of giving the dog small meals at regular intervals, he will give it all its daily food in one huge lump. The owner then promptly shuts the dog in the house and goes off to work for nine hours. It should be no surprise to find that the dog has made a mess by the time the owner returns – especially if the dog has not been trained to use newspapers as a toilet.

Remedial toilet training is much harder than teaching the dog as a puppy. It is going to be a long hard slog. You must learn to get things in the right order. First thing in the morning take the dog out to be toileted in the garden or gutter. If you cannot get out of the house make it use newspapers on the floor.

Patience is everything. You must wait until the dog has produced a result. Encourage it with a key-phrase such as "Get done" or "Do your stuff", and praise it warmly when it obliges. After a few weeks of consistent praise your dog will relieve itself when *you* say – provided you wait patiently for two or three minutes.

After early morning toileting, give the dog a small meal. When you leave for work leave newspapers on the kitchen floor where the dog can relieve itself if necessary. Restrict it to that part of the house.

In the early evening, give the dog a small meal – preferably by 6 pm. Last thing at night take it for a walk and wait patiently for it to relieve itself. Praise it when it succeeds.

If you do not have a garden, choose a quiet street and train the dog to toilet itself in the gutter. Make sure there is no traffic coming; many dogs have been killed in this way.

Never allow your dog to relieve itself on the pavement or in parks. This gives every dog owner a bad name. There is no excuse. If your dog has been allowed to get away with this in the past (and many owners encourage their dogs to do this) you must suddenly change your ways. The dog will not understand why it is suddenly being ticked off for doing what it has always done, but it will get the message if it meets with consistent disapproval – a yank on the chain and a shout of "Bad" as soon as it looks like doing the wrong thing. You must keep the dog moving until you have reached the appointed spot – whether it is a quiet roadside gutter or your garden.

Accidents will happen with hard-case dirty dogs. You must carry the means to clean up afterwards – after you have ticked the dog off. Pooper-scoopers are excellent devices – quick, clean and easy to use. They are large bags with a clip-fasten top. We would recommend you to take lots of kitchen roll with you as well to finish off the clean-up.

Dogs that urinate in the house usually have not been trained to relieve themselves on command. Such training may cure the problem. Also control the dog's liquid intake.

The pooper-scooper needs a steady nerve

There are some dogs which urinate through nervousness. This may be incurable, and the best you can do is to make sure there is always a corner of a room laid out with newspapers, so that you can drag the dog onto them when accidents start to happen. The dog may eventually go there naturally.

Finally, and most unpleasantly, some dogs eat their own faeces. In nearly every case, such dogs are suffering from a dietary deficiency. You should consult your vet who will advise you on the best dietary supplements for your pet.

DESTRUCTIVE DOGS

Destructive dogs are often the victims of their owners' stupidity. If you lock a dog in a house for an entire working day, and give it no toys to play with and nothing to chew, it should come as no surprise that it takes it out on the furniture and fittings.

Dogs need company as much as human beings. When they are left alone they get bored. They will amuse themselves in any way they can, and that includes chewing the wallpaper, the carpet, the three-piece suite or your best pair of shoes.

It is no use shouting at the dog when you come home, and pointing to the damage. The dog will not understand. The idea that a dog will remember what he did four hours ago, and connect that with the punishment you are now giving him, is entirely wrong. The dog will think he is being punished for something he has just done.

The only way to make the dog understand is to catch him in the act. This will need patience. If he chews the furniture, for example, you must lock him in the room where he does the damage and pretend to go out. You may have to rig up a mirror at the window to observe his behaviour. As soon as he chews the furniture, you should go into the room and give him a severe ticking off. Tell him he is "Bad"; attach a lead to his check-chain and give it a good pull.

With things like letters or shoes, it is much easier to catch your dog in the act. Leave him in a room with the temptation and keep looking in to see if he is up to his tricks. As soon as he does wrong, punish him.

You can, of course, prevent damage by giving the dog toys which you have encouraged him to play with – an old shoe or sock. Dogs love smelly, dirty things especially, and will usually prefer these to the objects you value.

If you have a garden, think about building a proper kennel, and provide your dog with toys. But make sure that he cannot get out of the garden and become a nuisance to traffic or to your neighbours. You may have to tether him on a long lead. A garden shed is often a good place for a dog to pass the day, provided there is enough room for him to move about, and again, provided you have given him plenty of toys.

If you do not have a garden, keep the dog in one room, and remove temptation. Those objects you cannot remove, like carpets, can be sprayed with "bitter apple" to make them repulsive to the dog. But above all you must provide toys to amuse him.

Indoor kennels are a last resort for anyone who does not have a garden. Buy the biggest you can reasonably afford, or convert a big cupboard into a kennel by caging the entrance – under stairs cupboards are often quite large. Make them light and airy, and fill them with toys. We do not think it fair to shut a dog in a kennel from 8 am to 6 pm with nothing to do, so if you have to resort to this, you must come home at lunchtime to give the dog some company and exercise.

NOISY DOGS

You cannot ignore a noisy dog. If you own one, you are likely to be a very unpopular neighbour. Even if you are out all day and are not bothered by the racket the dog makes, you owe it to the rest of humanity to shut it up.

It is a commonly held view that a barking dog is a bit of bad luck, something beyond your control. This is simply not true. In most cases, dogs can be silenced if their owners are prepared to put in time and effort to train them out of their bad habits.

The first thing you must sort out in your own mind is when you want your dog to bark, and when you want it to be quiet. A dog that barks at burglars is a useful protection. A dog that barks at an attacker in the street is a potential life-saver. It is obvious, then, that you do not want your pet to be completely silent all the time, but to stop barking when you tell it to stop. For this you will need a secret weapon – water.

Lock the dog in an outhouse or a shed, somewhere you know it usually barks when left alone. Arm yourself with a mug of cold water, and wait for the noise to begin.

As soon as the dog begins to bark, unlock the door, and tell it to be quiet. Think of a key-word that you will be able to use time and again in such circumstances. We simply shout "Quiet". If the dog continues to bark, throw the mug of water at it. Dogs hate water being thrown at them – they will do anything to escape it. You now have a harmless way of enforcing discipline.

Of course, your dog will soon get used to the threat of water, and will stop barking as soon as it hears a tap being turned on. This is not the object of the exercise. You are trying to get the dog to obey your command, rather than be quiet when it hears water running. You must therefore use stealth to keep the element of surprise. Fill old soft drink bottles with water, or jam jars, anything you have lying around. When the barking or the howling starts, conceal the water and approach the dog. Tell it to be quiet. Use the key-word chosen. When it disobeys, douse it. After a time, you can substitute a water pistol or an old plastic lemon juice bottle for the jam jars. The effect will be much the same.

Sooner or later, the dog will catch on that the best way to avoid a dousing is to obey your order to be quiet. It will always expect to be drenched, and you will soon be able to give the key-word to be quiet, without having to resort to using the water. When that point has been reached, you have a dog that will be silent on command.

A great many dogs are noisy only in very particular circumstances. Some bark at the telephone, or in cars for example. If you find it a nuisance, use the water treatment for that problem alone.

The most difficult noisy dog is the one that barks when you have gone out of the house. Here you will need to fill several jam jars with water ready for your return. You may have to stage-manage going out, to catch the dog in the act of barking. Pretend to set off for the shops, doing everything you normally do, including taking your bags. Then wait within earshot for the barking to start. As soon as it does, rush up to the dog, tell it to be quiet, and douse it with water. You will need to repeat this exercise several times before the message sinks in. If your neighbour bears the brunt of the dog's noise, bring him in on the water training, so that he too can order the dog to be quiet. Eventually the dog might take some notice of his voice as well.

AMOROUS DOGS

Dogs and sex can be quite a problem. Because they are pets, doing what comes naturally is not possible. They are domestic animals, and they have to fit in with your life. The owner decides the where, when, how and if of his dog's amorous adventures. This is a recipe for delinquency of all kinds.

Dogs – the male of the species that is – can be an embarrassing nuisance around legs; all shapes, sizes and sexes of leg, and all of them human. It is a common sight to see small human beings mounted in the most ungainly way by large dogs, and large human beings trying desperately to shake off a small amorous male dog which has taken a fancy to their lower leg.

Some dogs do this because they are young and frustrated. Sheer excitement can set a young dog off. Pull him away and calm him down if he still tries to mate with your visitor's leg. Pull him away and give him a slap on the nose. Tell him he is bad. If after a few months, his behaviour has not improved, more drastic action must be considered.

Think about castration. If you do not intend to breed from your dog, it may be the kindest course of action – both to save embarrassment and your dog the constant threat of being ticked off. Even if you have a pedigree dog, breeding may be unwise if it shows severe behaviour problems.

Of course castration will not cure your dog's other most likely form of sexual delinquency – interfering with the parts of human beings that most humans would prefer them not to reach. Dogs of both sexes do this. It is part of their normal behaviour.

They smell each other, and can see no reason why they should not smell you. They tend to go for the places that smell most interesting to them, and that can be embarrassing for humans. Unfortunately women come off worse here, simply because skirts and dresses are easier targets than trousers. It is not that male dogs find women more interesting than men. In fact dogs and bitches seem to be completely undiscriminating about this. To them a smell is just a smell. It is either interesting or it is not. The wearer of that smell is immaterial.

The solution is much the same as before. The dog should be dragged away and told he is "Bad". He will soon get the idea, even though his desire to smell remains strong.

Bitches on heat can be a nuisance. They will try to get out of the house, out of the garden, out of the car – anything to meet dogs who are interested in mating. You can be invaded by dozens of dogs who have been smitten by the scent of romance. Separating bitch from dog can be painful – for you. Your actions may be met by aggression from both parties.

The only certain cure for your problems is to have your bitch sterilised by the vet. The canine term is spayed. Most vets prefer

to carry out the operation between the bitch's first and second seasons. There are few side effects, other than a tendency to put on weight in old age.

Bitches that have given birth may be very snappy when you approach their puppies. This is not a delinquency problem, merely maternal instinct. When the puppies are a few weeks old, the bitch will return to her old self.

ROAD HOG DOGS

Every driver knows the problem: a dog appears out of nowhere and dashes in front of your car. There is no sign of an owner. The dog is completely out of control and a risk to every road user's life. Worse still are the dogs who chase cars or cyclists, because unless they are brought under control they are certain to cause an accident sooner or later.

There can be no sympathy at all for owners who let their dogs run wild in the street. If they claim that the dog runs away, and there is nothing they can do to get it back, they are simply making excuses. There are plenty of ways of training a dog to come when it is called, before it even reaches the temptation of the open road. We will show you how to do this in Chapter 4.

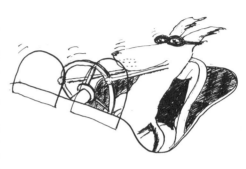

However, a dog that has become addicted to playing in traffic is extremely difficult to cure. You must keep it away from roads for its own good, as well as the good of motorists. We have known dogs that have been run over several times, and yet still chase cars, such is the extent of their addiction. Sam, the Labrador-Alsatian cross which took part in the Reform School was just such a case. His owner did not have the sense to lock him up before she went out, nor did she have the control of her pet to make him come when he was called. The result was that Sam was free to chase not only any car that passed in the street, but his owner's car as well. Astonishing as it may seem, Sam's owner had actually developed a game of racing the dog in her own car. She saw it as the only way to leave home without running over the dog. She was wrong. Sam was run over by his owner only a few days before the Reform School course began.

Certain breeds of dog are worse traffic nuisances than others. Collies, for example, have been bred to herd sheep, and find it very tempting to do the same thing with cars and bicycles. If they are persistent offenders, it may be possible to cure them with cold water.

You should stage-manage corrective treatment, rather than wait for it to happen. For bicycle-chasing dogs, you will need two people on bikes, a quiet road, preferably off the public highway, water pistols, and as a back-up, several plastic containers of water.

First, arm your bicycle riders with water, preferably out of sight of the dog. Then arrange for the dog to see the riders come past. The riders should try to excite the dog, so that it is tempted to chase. Holding the dog on a lead (preferably a long lead – you may have to attach some rope to your ordinary lead) let the dog follow his natural instincts. If he chases, the riders should wait their opportunity, and drench the dog. You can follow up with your own mug of water, and a firm scolding. You should repeat the exercise at hourly, or half-hourly intervals to allow the dog time to forget. If you do this for several weeks, a couple of days every week, the dog will begin to get the message that bicycle-chasing is not much fun.

The same technique can be applied to dogs that chase cars. Again, set up the training situation away from a public road. This time, a passenger in the car should be armed with a water pistol. You should have the dog on a long lead, and as soon as bad behaviour starts, the car should stop, and both you and the passenger should drench the dog.

There will always be some dogs too addicted to car-chasing for even water to deter. As with all dogs, prevention is the best way of stopping them being a nuisance. Never give them the opportunity to go near the road off the lead. It may be difficult when your local park is next to a main road, for example. If you cannot guarantee that your dog will come when it is called, run with it on its lead to give it its daily exercise, or change parks.

SHY DOGS

Dogs are shy for two reasons: either they are nervous through breeding faults, or they have not learned how to socialise.

With inbred nervousness, there is little you can do by way of training them out of their shyness. Such dogs are genuinely afraid of strange noises, strange faces, strange places. You have to learn to live with the dog's limitations – and the restrictions that puts on your life, or you must find a friend or neighbour who can. As a last resort, you must consider having the dog put down by the vet.

With unsocialised dogs, it may simply be a question of getting them used to company – the company of humans and other dogs. If you have cut them off from the outside world, for whatever reason, you will have to take their rehabilitation very gently. Rocky was just such a dog on the Reform School course, and he found a crowd of other dogs and owners very intimidating at first. Up until then, his owner had kept him away from other people in the mistaken belief that this would make Rocky a better guard-dog, one that would drive intruders away. In reality, Rocky was so unused to seeing other humans that he did not know how to react.

With dogs like this, it is important to make human beings seem friendly. When you introduce the dog to people, make sure you have given them some tit-bits for him. It would be a good idea to take the dog along to a training course, since that will give you something to do while the dog gets used to other people. Do not rush your dog. If you do, you could make him aggressive through fear, and you will have simply added to his problems.

TEARAWAY DOGS

By tearaway, we mean dogs that pull on their leads, dragging their owners along behind them. If you own a small dog, this may not seem much of a problem, but we have met owners who find their large dogs so troublesome that they dare not take them out for a walk for fear of being pulled into the path of a car.

You will have to be tough if you are to control a big dog that has been allowed to get away with being a tearaway. You may need help from someone stronger than yourself, someone who can physically dominate the dog until he has learned his lesson.

Before you start, make sure you have the right equipment to carry out the task. As we mentioned in the section dealing with aggressive dogs, you need the right kind of lead. It should be made of leather to give you a good grip. The lead should be attached to a strong, fine-link check-chain. The chain should pass round the dog's neck and come up behind its left ear. This is because the correct side for your dog to walk is by your left leg. If you were to walk with the dog beside your right leg with the check-chain still behind the dog's left ear, you might well cause the dog distress, because the chain can easily snag. If you are unsure about which way the check-chain should slide, slip the noose over your hand and pull it over your forearm. Make sure that it goes slack as soon as you release the tension on the chain.

Your strong friend should take the dog, and be prepared to check him as soon as he starts to pull. This will almost certainly happen within the first few steps. He should give the dog a quick jerk on the check-chain, and tell him he is bad. He should order the dog to "Heel" using the key-word loudly and firmly, pulling tight on the check-chain at the same time until the dog is in position.

The dog will almost certainly object, and might even try to bite. So long as the handler keeps his hand high up the lead, and the check-chain tight, there is no possibility of the dog's biting. He should walk on, keeping the dog firmly by his left leg, and ordering him to heel.

As soon as the dog stops pulling, he should be praised. Tell him he is a "Good boy". If he continues to walk to heel, the check-chain should be relaxed and the praise should continue – coupled with a repetition of the key-word "Heel". After a while, you should take over, and follow the same procedure. You should not be afraid to use the check-chain whenever the dog pulls, gradually releasing it as he begins to obey. Always tell him he is bad when he does things wrong, and tell him he is a good boy when he does them right.

If you do not have access to a strong friend, you can always carry a rolled up newspaper with you as an extra sanction. When the dog pulls, give a strong yank on the check-chain, tell him he is bad, and reinforce the message with a tap on the nose. Then repeat the key-word "Heel" and start all over again.

RUNAWAY DOGS

Dogs that run away in the park when you want them to come, dogs that abscond from home when you have told them to stay form one of the biggest single delinquency categories of all. They must be taught to come when they are called – not just when they feel like coming.

For this you may need to arm yourself with a reward – lumps of cheese, pieces of grilled liver or chicken, choc drops, anything the dog really enjoys as a treat. You will also need a 30-foot rope to attach to your lead and check-chain, so that the dog can be given limited freedom to misbehave.

Choose a wide open space like a park, and attach the long lead. Let the dog wander off about ten feet at first and then call him. Use his name: "Rover, come". If the dog responds, praise him warmly and let him wander off again.

Repeat the process until the dog decides not to come. You may have to give him a fair bit of rope for this to happen. As soon as he disobeys, give a sharp pull on the rope – not a half-hearted affair, a full-blooded tug. If he fails to come on the second call, don't repeat yourself; walk up to your dog, tell him he is "Bad" several times and yank his check-chain.

You then repeat the process, giving him twenty feet of rope and calling him to you using the same key-phrase.

The secret is to give the dog only one firm command rather than repeating yourself. When he disobeys yank the check-chain and tell him off. Make your voice harsh and really shout at him: "Bad, bad".

Sooner or later, he will get the idea. The first time he comes, you must praise him wildly. Do not stint – hug him, kiss him, give him a tit-bit and keep repeating your praise. It will sink into his skull that he has just learned the most wonderful trick in the world. All he does is come when he is called, and the world suddenly is a different place, one in which he is petted and given his favourite food.

Try this for a couple of hours on the first day. It will be hard work. After a few weeks you should be able to risk letting him off the lead altogether. You will have established in the dog's mind that running off when his owner calls is wrong. Your voice alone will tell him so. He will genuinely want to come.

If it does not work, you will have to put him back on the rope, and start again.

FOOD FADDY DOGS

Dogs which are faddy about food are often encouraged in their delinquency by over-indulgent owners. If you have allowed your dog to become over-fussy about what he eats, you must start again at square one, and do what you should have done when the dog was a puppy.

First, you should learn what your dog really needs to eat every day to stay healthy. That means not only the kind of food, but the quantity as well. In our buyer's guide at the back of this book, we give you a rough guide to the quantity of food a dog needs, breed by breed. Consult your local breeders for specific dietary advice.

When you know what your dog should be eating, do not take no for an answer. If the dog turns up his nose at your offering, take it away and give him nothing for another hour. Then place the same food before him. Dogs are not stupid. They will sooner eat something they do not care for than starve.

Do not give your dog chocolate drops, or chocolate biscuits all day as a treat. These are anything but treats to the dog's digestive system and teeth and they get it into bad habits. Treats should be reserved for when the dog has done something exceptional, and the best treat is healthy food like a biscuit or a small lump of cheese or meat.

DOGS IN CARS

There are a hundred ways for a dog to make a nuisance of itself in a car. By far the worst is the dog that interferes with your driving, making you into a traffic hazard. A dog should never be allowed to roam around in the passenger compartment of a car, no matter how well trained it is. Dogs have a tendency to react to events outside the car without thinking where they are. A dog can easily go through the windscreen of a car in pursuit of a cat or another dog, or in its attempt to greet a member of the family it has seen on the pavement. It is up to you to prevent it doing itself damage, and possibly causing an accident.

There are a number of car cages on the market. Some work better than others. We have come across several instances of the ineffectiveness of the telescopic bar kind of restraint, usually installed in hatchback and estate cars to confine the dog to the luggage compartment. Crafty dogs can squeeze their heads between the side of the car and the bars, creating a gap through which to climb. If you brake suddenly, the first thing you know of your dog's antics is the sight of him flying forwards.

Better, but much more expensive, are the fully-fitted car cages, which can be anchored to the sides of the car. These can be made quite comfortable for the dog, and many pets feel more secure in them because they stop them being thrown around inside the car.

In saloon cars, it is much more difficult to install a cage or bars without cramping the passenger compartment and making it difficult to use when the dog is not travelling with you. Here, and for hatchback and estate cars as well, we would recommend the cheapest solution of all – metal hooks soldered into the side of the car in the rear compartment. The dogs can be tethered reasonably tightly, so that they cannot interfere with your driving, but with enough leeway to keep them comfortable.

Some dogs are travel sick. This can be a very annoying and messy problem, but the solution may be easier than you think. There seems to be a link between static electricity in a car interior and a dog's feelings of queasiness. If you spread newspaper on the seat and floor where the dog is likely to sit, it should go a long way to solving the problem because it acts as a kind of earth. It has the added advantage of making cleaning up a lot easier if accidents do happen. An anti-static trailing bar might be worth fitting to the underside of your car if the problem persists.

Dogs that howl or bark in cars are too numerous to be funny. Often dogs make most noise when a journey is about to end. Many go berserk when they hear the car indicators going, because they think the driver is about to turn into their street or drive. Sometimes the dog may be right. More often, the indicators will not be signalling the end of a journey, and unless you do something to stop the noise, you will be saddled with it for good. The only solution is to stage-manage a journey simply for the purpose of silencing the dog. Have a passenger douse it with water from a water pistol and use the check-chain every time the noise starts. It might be an idea to tie the dog down near the floor of the car so that it cannot see out of the windows. This will make the journey less interesting for your pet, but, with a bit of luck, a lot quieter for you.

Finally, never let a dog lean out of an open car window. We see dozens of cars where this is allowed to happen, and no matter what the drivers say, the dog is not fully under control. If there isn't a law against it, there should be.

CHILD-HATING DOGS

Very few dogs really hate children. It is usually the children who are the cause of any friction, and the reason you have blamed the dog is because you have failed to notice how bad your children are.

Ask yourself why your dog is apparently well-behaved for you, and occasionally vicious with your children. When does the viciousness happen? Is there any pattern to it? Has there been a change in the family circumstances that could have brought about new tensions?

Dogs can cause jealousy in children in the same way as new babies can. If you have bought a dog for the children, and seem to be giving it a lot of attention – the kind of attention any conscientious new owner should give – then one of your children may feel left out. The child may start to tease the dog in an apparently playful way, while really trying to hurt the dog. We have seen parents blissfully unaware of their children, as the family dog is pulled and punched out of sight. The first thing the parent knows is that the dog has bitten the child in self-defence, and the child is calling for comfort and attention.

There will always be a reason for a dog to misbehave with one member of the family and not the rest. Some dogs dislike babies that cry. They may be jealous of all the attention the baby is getting. If this is the case, keep the dog away from the baby until the child is older. Tell it off, every time you think it is getting too near. The dog will find it easier to ignore the child than to try to like it.

Some children, usually younger members of the family, can be very insensitive to a dog's feelings, yet the dog gets the blame because the parent invariably sides with the child. Take, for example, the case of the child that sees the dog asleep in front of the fire, and out of affection dives on top of it in the hope that it will play. The first thing the dog knows is that it has been woken up suddenly by something threatening. It bites in self-defence. The child will complain to the parent that the dog has bitten him, claiming that he was only asking the dog to play. This may be the truth as the child sees it, especially if he thought the dog was awake. You will have to be vigilant from

then on to make sure your child does not invite more trouble.

It is a good idea to teach your dog and children not to be too boisterous in their play. They may both learn bad habits, which will be hard work to correct. The child must have a certain respect for the dog, and should follow your example in not getting it over-excited.

It is foolish to think that a child under the age of ten or eleven can really be responsible for a dog. It is human nature for children of that age to forget to feed or exercise the family pet, even though the dog is officially their dog. You can encourage the child to take as much responsibility as possible, but discreetly, in the background, you are always in charge. It is a game of kidology, but it is vital if the dog is to be well looked after.

Finally, do not encourage your dog to lick the children's faces. One day, the dog will have just been rooting in some filthy dustbin when he decides to take a lick.

THIEVING DOGS

There are few dogs that will not steal if the temptation is great enough. Put a freshly cooked joint of meat within easy striking range, then leave the room, and what dog could resist a nibble? For that matter, how is a dog supposed to know that you have not put the meat out for him?

Food is the biggest problem when it comes to dogs and theft. Prevention is the answer rather than cure. Of course, if you have allowed things to reach the point where the dog is stealing things from the table where you are eating, you will need to start from scratch and teach it basic remedial table manners.

The dog must know when you want it to eat and when you want it to leave food alone. Start with its daily feeding. First, put the lead and check-chain on the dog, then fill his bowl with food. When he has had a few mouthfuls, tell him to "Leave", and take the bowl away. If the dog tries to reach the bowl, tell him he is "Bad" and correct him with a yank on the check-chain. Repeat the command "Leave", and make the dog know by your voice that you mean it. We call that "putting your voice on the dog". Under no circumstances should you give the dog his food once you have told him to leave it. This will confuse him. You must leave the room with the dog and wait a few minutes before going on to the next stage.

With the dog in another room, return to the kitchen or the place where the dog is normally fed. Place the bowl of food on the floor once more. Then bring the dog in, making sure he is still on a lead with a check-chain. Let the dog eat a few mouthfuls, and then tell him to leave the food. Use the key-word "Leave!", as your command. If he fails to leave the food, correct him with the check-chain and the key-word "Bad!".

You may have to repeat this exercise many times over several days or even weeks before the dog eventually learns that when you say "Leave!", you mean it. In the meantime, you must prevent the dog from getting his own way with food in other circumstances. All tit-bits are out, for the time being, and that means tit-bits from any member of the family, not just from you. The dog should not be allowed near the table where you are eating, so that the temptation to snatch food does not arise.

Only when you are sure that the dog has learned his lesson, and genuinely leaves food when you tell him to – without the lead and check-chain – only then should normal life resume.

Any sign that the dog is going back to his old ways should be clamped down on firmly. But you must also avoid tempting the dog. It is hopeless for one member of your family to keep slipping the dog tit-bits

from the table, while you are being very strict on enforcing the table as a no-go area where dogs and food are concerned.

Do not be lulled into a false sense of security after your dog has just had his official feed. In the wild, dogs eat as much as they can after they have made a kill. It is their way of stocking up for the hard time that might lie ahead. Domestic dogs will also continue to eat as though they do not know where their next meal is coming from – unless you prevent them.

Other kinds of theft, such as dogs which steal slippers or washing from the line, are dealt with in exactly the same way as we taught you to treat the problems of destructiveness in dogs earlier.

PREVENTING DELINQUENCY

Prevention is not only better than cure, it is also much less hard work. By the time a dog needs the Reform School treatment, it may be too late. Old dogs *do* learn new tricks, but given half a chance they will slip back into their old ways. If your delinquent dog is more than three years old, you will be in for an uphill struggle, not least because you will probably have to undergo a change of personality yourself. After years of being a soft touch, you will suddenly need to transform yourself into a strict and often unlikeable sergeant-major. Your friends will not recognise you, especially since they will feel the lash of your tongue should they encourage your dog to return to its bad habits.

If, after trying out the Reform School methods outlined in this book, your delinquent pet proves too set in its ways to reform, learn from your mistakes. Next time you buy a dog (and in our experience most owners of delinquent dogs fail time and time again), try to get things right from the start. Here is how.

First, and this may seem blindingly obvious, choose the right breed of dog for your home circumstances. It is astonishing how many people, without the time or space to look after a big dog, go out and buy the biggest hound they can find. A Great Dane in a bedsitter is destined to become a delinquent dog, no matter how responsible its owner may try to be.

In our buyer's guide at the back of this book, we give details of the special needs of all common breeds. Read it carefully before deciding which kind of dog you would like. Do not go simply for the dog's looks; beauty is only fur deep, and will begin to pall after a few months of foul behaviour. Remember, dogs live for between ten and fifteen years, and it is much more important to choose a dog for its ability to fit in with your life than anything else.

Consider the following points before selecting your breed.

1. The size of your home
2. The size of your garden
3. Small children in the family
4. The time a dog needs for exercise
5. The time it needs for grooming
6. The cost of feeding the dog

CHOOSING A NON-DELINQUENT DOG

Once you have matched the breed to the limitations of your home and work patterns, choose a reputable breeder. There is usually a breed society in your area; telephone the secretary and ask for recommendations. Ask your vet and the Kennel Club as well. Always see at least two breeders, so that you can compare their methods and puppies. A good breeder will willingly show you the parents of the puppies you are interested in, and any of the puppies' other relations he or she may own. This is a good guide to the temperament of the dog in later years. The points to look for especially are any signs of nervousness or aggression in the adult dogs which might indicate breeding faults.

Once you are satisfied that the puppies do not suffer from breeding faults, choose the best puppy from that litter. With the breeder's consent, try the following experiment:

Ask the breeder to put all the puppies in the same room. Fuss all the dogs for a few minutes, then suddenly clap your hands as loudly as you can. The puppies will all rush to escape. Look to see which puppy is the first out of the door, or seems to respond fastest.

Wait and watch to see which is the first puppy to come back into the room. This is the one you are looking for. If it was also one of the first to leave when the hands were clapped, that is the puppy which is likely to respond best to training. Repeat the experiment later if the results are inconclusive at first. You will soon see how the puppies differ in their responses. Avoid the shy puppy that is too frightened to come back into the room to see what caused the noise.

Make sure the puppies are de-loused and de-wormed. You can see a thick brown dandruff on the puppy's skin if lice are present. Check for fleas by running your fingers the wrong way through its coat. You should be able to see them jump.

Male puppies are usually more trouble than females in terms of delinquency – they have much more natural aggression, though curiously, they are much more popular. If you do not intend to breed, a

Choose a reputable dealer

bitch spayed after its first season is a very much better bet.

If you are determined to buy a cross-breed instead of a pedigree animal, you are taking a big gamble. You cannot tell how it is likely to behave unless you see both parents. If that still does not put you off go to the RSPCA rather than a pet shop. Do not buy a grown dog which may have had habits ingrained – always go for a puppy, and try the hand-clap test we have just described.

If you have any reservations, do not buy. Wait a few months. There will always be another litter from the breeder you like.

BRINGING THE DOG HOME

Make sure you arrive at the breeder's a couple of hours before the dog's feeding time so that it is less likely to be sick on its first journey home.

Lay newspapers down in the kitchen so that it can relieve itself when it arrives. Carry paper towels with you in the car, just in case.

Many puppies are terrified on their first night alone. Do not be tempted to get into bad habits by taking it to bed with you. Comfort it by filling its basket with a warm hot water bottle inside a couple of old sweaters. Place a ticking clock inside the parcel. This will imitate the heat generated by the litter the puppy has just left and the heart beat of the other puppies.

Many puppies are terrified on their first night alone

In the first 16 weeks the puppy should not be allowed out of the house, for fear of picking up diseases from other dogs. Vaccinations start at 8 to 10 weeks and continue until the 16th week.

KEEPING DELINQUENT CHILDREN AT BAY

Children will often do their best to make a puppy delinquent in spite of your best efforts. Young children sometimes become jealous of the attention the puppy is getting and are capable of great cruelty.

Once a dog's confidence in children has been broken, it is never easy to win back.

First impress on your children how frail the puppy is. Its bones are very soft, and very young children should not even attempt to pick it up. Adults should do so with great care, placing the index finger between the front legs, using the thumb to support one leg and the rest of the hand to hold the other leg in check. Then with the other hand, support the puppy's rear end and gently lift it up.

You must allow your children to share in the care of the puppy in ways that will not bring about harm. Let them give him a drink, or a bowl of food, or tuck him up in bed at night. But always keep a watchful eye open.

HOUSE TRAINING

We have already mentioned the use of newspapers as an indoor toilet when the puppy comes home with you for the first time. Unless you have a really secluded garden, you cannot let the puppy out of the house safely until the vaccinations have been completed; so you must continue this practice for the first four months of the puppy's life.

You must therefore work out the best way of organising your life around this daily ritual.

First choose the room. Most people use the kitchen because it is near the back door, and is one step removed from the next stage in the dog's toilet training – the garden.

Do not wait for your puppy to choose his own time to use the toilet, take him to the allocated place and encourage him to go. Timing is crucial, but not very difficult to get right. Ten minutes after every meal or drink, most puppies are ready to go. Even if they show no inclination, take them. You can train them to relieve themselves on command.

You should have laid out newspapers over a large area – aim is not a puppy's strong point – and you should be prepared to stay and wait for a long time. You must be in the room with the dog. When success looks near you should be ready with words of encouragement. Think of a key-phrase you will be able to use in future such as "Good boy, get done", or "Good boy, get clean". When he succeeds, you must praise him again, even to the extent of hugging and stroking him so that he knows he's done something right. The more lavish your praise, the quicker he will learn. Of course, he will not *understand*, but he will respond. Every time he goes through his toileting successfully, repeat the key-phrase you have chosen to praise him.

It can take several weeks of repeating this exercise for the message to strike home properly, but if you work hard at it, you could see results after about a week. Even if the whole process seems tedious, think how much more tedious it will be in coming years, when you have to clear up mess after mess simply because the dog has been allowed to get his own way.

If you have a garden, even a small garden, it is far better to make use of this than somewhere inside. If you are lucky enough to have no other dogs in the neighbourhood, or if you know for certain that no other dogs can get into your garden, you will be able to train your puppy to use the garden from the start, even before vaccination. Choose one small section of the garden as the regular place for toileting. The method of training is the same as for indoors.

Under no circumstances should your dog get used to relieving himself in the park, or worse still, in the street. There is no one more selfish than the dog owner who tries to keep his own garden free from mess by dumping his problem outside his neighbour's front gate. It is *your* dog, and *you* must take responsibility for its behaviour.

TABLE MANNERS

Like children, dogs have to be taught that feeding is not just re-fuelling. It involves more than one person. There is the person who makes the meal and has to watch it being consumed, and there is the hungry consumer. Both parties' feelings have to be taken into account.

The first rule is that the dog eats when *you* want him to eat, and not before. Do not allow him to jump up at you as you prepare the food. Teach him to sit and wait – we will show you how, later in the book. When you are ready, tell him: "Good boy, have your dinner now."

Dogs must be taught when to stop eating as well as when to start. There is a good reason for this. The day may dawn when your allegedly obedient dog spots a dustbin full of tempting food. This is the moment when he decides to come out in his true delinquent colours. You must be able to part him from a succulent chicken carcase without losing a finger. For this reason, you must get the dog used to having his food taken away. This should never be done to tease the dog, just to teach him a lesson. When he is young, take his dish from him after he has started feeding. If there are any signs of aggression, give him a little shake and tell him off. Tell him: "Bad, bad". Return the dish and try again. If his aggression persists, take away the food and repeat the telling-off. You are getting the dog used to the idea that if you want to withdraw the dish, he must be prepared to let you.

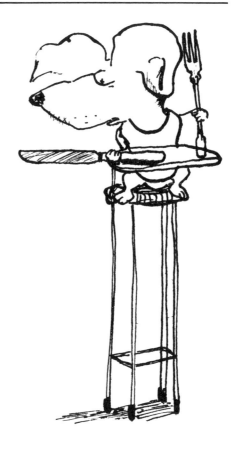

THE FIRST OUTING

You should prepare for the day of the first outing from the time you buy your puppy. It is going to be a shock, so he had better be ready.

First, get him used to wearing a collar from the first day in the house. Buy a very thin cat's collar and make him wear it around the home. This may take time, but it will avoid tantrums when you put on a full-sized collar later. Leave this thin collar on for about five minutes on the first day, and gradually increase the time day by day. Because puppies grow quickly, you may have to buy more than one collar, so don't buy anything expensive.

You must take much more care in choosing the puppy's full-sized collar. It should be made of soft leather, and the ideal size is just big enough to slip two fingers between the collar and the neck.

This will be neither too tight for comfort, nor too big to slip off, and it will be able to take an identity disc for your name, address and phone number, should the dog ever be lost. It is not a good idea to put the dog's name on the identity disc as well as your own name. There have been unfortunate cases where two people claim ownership of a lost dog. If you can get the dog to respond to its name, you can prove that *you* are the rightful owner – provided you haven't left things too late. If the dog has been lost for a long time, it may like its new name better.

Most puppies do not need a check-chain for their first walk. An ordinary leather collar will be enough to keep them under control. Bigger, more boisterous dogs may need a check-chain to stop them dragging their owners along. The ideal chain should be good quality steel with a reasonably fine link. The chain should fit comfortably round the dog's neck, but should not be loose enough to catch the dog's forelegs when it is slack. When you put the chain around the dog's neck, make sure that you attach the lead on the left hand side of the dog. These chains are designed to slide one way, and if you put them onto the dog incorrectly, they can trap the dog's skin, causing great pain. The choice of lead is also of great importance. It should be a strong leather lead with a strong clip.

Once you have assembled all your props, you are ready to take your dog out for its first walk. It is here that delinquent patterns of behaviour can begin. If he resists violently against the idea of being on a lead, do not try to force him. Take him home and get him used to a lead in the house. Tie a short piece of string to his collar and practise leading him about, a little at a time. It is far better to have mini-tantrums on the carpet than on the pavement where a puppy's footpads can be easily skinned. Gradually, you will get your dog used to being on the lead, and he will realise that going for a walk is fun. Many dogs are a bit scared of traffic or sudden noises, or the unexpected appearance of a cat. If he tries to bolt, hold him firmly on the lead and reassure him. Never let your dog off the lead near traffic, because one of these sudden happenings could make him jump into the path of traffic. This rule applies even to well-trained dogs.

BASIC OBEDIENCE

1) Coming when Called

This is the toughest lesson for the would-be delinquent dog to learn. It often means forcing the dog to give up the thing he would like to do most, in order to fit in with what *you* want to do. It causes tantrums in children; it causes as many tantrums in dogs.

Place your dog in a room and close all the doors behind you to cut off his means of escape. Keep a tit-bit hidden until the dog is on the other side of the room. Then using a key-phrase which includes the dog's name, say quietly "Rover, come". Try to sound enthusiastic, as if there is a reward about to be given. Show the dog the reward. When he comes, first lavish praise on him, then give him his reward. At this stage, it is not essential for the dog to sit when he comes.

During the course of an evening, repeat this exercise two or three times, always

Call his name quietly

SPOT!!

using the key-phrase "Rover, come", and always giving the dog his reward. No dog likes to miss out on a treat, and even dogs with delinquent tendencies should soon respond well.

Make things slightly more difficult. Give the dog the freedom of a couple of rooms, still closing off the escape routes. When you are in one room, and the dog is in another, call him. You may have to repeat yourself quite a few times before he responds. Whatever you do, do not lose patience and tick him off for failing to come. All you will have succeeded in doing is in cancelling the reward principle you have just gone to so much trouble to establish.

If the dog fails to come, go back to using one room again. Only when you have succeeded many times to get the dog to come, should you risk punishing him for being slow to respond to your call. If he decides to run off when you call, go after him and tell him off, using the key-word "Bad". Walk away from him and tell him to come once more, offering him his tit-bit. If he fails to come, go after him again and tell him he is "Bad". Keep repeating the exercise until he comes, and remember to be generous with your praise when he gets things right. It may take several weeks of home training for the message to get firmly into the dog's head, but by doing it indoors you are not risking your dog running off into traffic or any of the other hazards of the outside world. Dogs who run off are just about the most common kind of delinquent around.

2) Getting the Dog to Stay

You need only go on to this lesson when the puppy is older. We think puppies up to the age of about four months should have only enough training to ensure their basic safety. After their puppyhood, however, you can go on to teach them a whole range of lessons which will make living with them very much easier.

Teaching a dog to sit and stay is probably the most useful thing you will ever do with him. If he responds to order, you need never worry about a whole range of bad habits, such as jumping up at strangers who come to your house. A firm command of "Sit, stay!" should be enough to prevent such behaviour before it begins.

As before, it is easier if you start this training in the house. First, get the dog to sit by saying firmly "Sit!", and at the same time press the dog's hindquarters firmly down. At first, only your hand will achieve the result you want. But by constant repetition of the key-phrases "Good boy!" when the dog stays seated, and "Bad!"

when he stands up, he will soon get the message about what to do to earn praise. You do not need tit-bits to succeed. Your praise is the biggest incentive a dog can have.

As with teaching the dog to come when called, teaching him to sit may take a few weeks of constant repetition. When he has got the hang of it, you can go on to the next, more important stage – staying on command.

You should go through the routine of getting the dog to sit, as before. But this time, you intend to leave him instead of staying by his side. Say firmly "Sit, stay!", keeping eye contact with the dog. Wait until you are sure he has taken the command in, and then slowly move backwards away from him, still maintaining eye contact. Keep repeating the key-phrase: "Sit, stay!" all the time. If the dog begins to stand up, go back to him and tell him off by saying "Bad!", and ordering him to sit once more. You may have to make him sit. Then repeat the exercise of standing in front of him and beginning to walk backwards away from him. Don't go too far at first. When your dog succeeds in staying in the seated position, begin to walk back towards him, still saying the key-phrase: "Sit, stay!". Again, if he gets up, tell him he is bad and start all over again.

Eventually, you will succeed in returning to your dog while he remains seated. Tell him that his lesson is over by using the key-word: "Finish!", and then give him lots of praise. It will take a great many repetitions before you get a consistent response.

After a time, you will be able to walk further and further away while your dog sits and stays. Each time, walk back to him, reinforcing the message: "Sit, stay!", and maintaining eye contact. You are now ready to combine this lesson with Lesson One. For this you will probably need a reward in the form of a piece of cheese. When you have retreated some twenty yards from your dog, stop, take out the cheese and hold it in the palm of your hand. Then tell your dog to come, using the key-phrase which includes his name: "Rover, come!", or whatever. After all the hours of teaching him to stay where he is, he may be a little anxious. That is what the reward is for. Sound as encouraging as you can, and eventually he should come.

When he arrives, it is a good idea to make him sit before he is given the reward of food. This is especially important with big, boisterous dogs. The extra discipline you get by making him wait is good for teaching the dog how to control his excitement. When he sits, give him the cheese, tell him the lesson is over by the key-word "Finish!" and then give him lots of praise. As with all these lessons, you should eventually be able to do without food as a reward; your praise will be enough.

Once your dog has mastered the basics of sitting and staying, you can apply the lesson to everyday situations in the home. When you arrive home, instead of allowing the dog to jostle you at the front door (something very annoying if you are carrying shopping), get him to sit and stay until you have opened the door. When you are inside, and when you have put your bags down, only then should you tell him to come. Praise him for doing as he is told. If you want him to sit while you put away your shopping, tell him to do so, and do not take no for an answer. You must be consistent for your dog to understand that he will be rewarded when he does things right, and punished when he does them wrongly.

We have already mentioned table manners. Getting your dog to sit and wait until you have put his food into the dish is a good lesson in control, and makes things easier for you. In the end, your dog will be happier, because his world is secure, and you will be happier, knowing that you can have the pleasure of both an affectionate and obedient dog.

3) Walking to Heel

Already we are beyond the first stage of teaching a dog basic obedience. But making your pet walk to heel will make him much more of a pleasure when you go into busy traffic, or crowded places, anywhere where you do not want a dog either dragging you along by the lead, or lagging behind to inspect some item of interest.

The method of training is much the same as before. First, you must have control of your dog so that you can correct any mistakes he makes. A lead, with a check-chain attached, is essential. You must practise walking to heel in controlled situations. Remember your dog does not understand what you mean when you shout "Heel!". You must teach him by shouting the key-word and pulling him into position. If he pulls in front, give him a good sharp pull on the check-chain and shout "Bad". Bring him to the right position – as near as possible to your left calf – and set off walking once more, slowly at first, and holding the dog on a tight rein. Gradually release your grip, and praise the dog as long as he stays close to you. As soon as he starts to pull forwards or back, tighten your grip once more and repeat the key-word "Heel". Once your dog is in the right position again tell him he is a "Good boy". When he goes astray, tell him he is "Bad" and pull him back into position. Then repeat the command "Heel".

Dogs do not understand the word 'heel'

As with all similar lessons, it will take possibly weeks of reinforcing the message before your dog walks to heel without too much fuss, and on command. The secret is to choose the time and place when you want to teach the dog new tricks, not wait until the need for control arises and find that your dog fails to obey.

THE BUYER'S GUIDE TO DELINQUENT DOGS

The following guide is not intended to help you to choose a delinquent dog, but to avoid buying one. The pitfalls are many. Just when you think you have seen the most beautiful dog in the world at the top of the page, you will find that it will either eat your children, or eat you out of house and home. We have tried to make your task easier by recommending good buys for several sizes of dog.

However, only you know your home circumstances and what will suit you best. We have heard of one man who has a huge Newfoundland in a maisonette. The dog goes with him every day to work, and follows him as he goes from job to job. No one could predict that such an arrangement would have the slightest chance of working. You may be able to make similar unusual adjustments. We wish you good luck.

A word of explanation about the summary at the foot of each page. It is a rough guide to enable you to compare dog with dog at a glance. Housing needs refer to the space a dog needs to be happiest, and are only an approximate guide. Exercise needs mean the amount of exercise your dog needs once it has reached the park for its run *off the lead*. The walk to and from the park does not count. Grooming needs are the minimum time you must groom your dog to avoid annoying hair-loss on furniture and clothes. This may not worry you; if so, you may be able to get away with less. Food costs can only be a very rough guide, since the size of dogs varies so much. Consult local breeders about the feeding of the breed you choose.

 DELINQUENCY RATING

 HOUSING NEEDS

 EXERCISE NEEDS

 GROOMING NEEDS

 FOOD COSTS

Some Afghans are worn rather than owned – dragged along by fashionable owners, who want to be noticed. This is a great pity, because it can be a very desirable pet if owners take it seriously.

It is a huge dog – around 28 inches tall and very slender – and takes up a great deal of time in exercise and grooming. In wet weather it can easily take a couple of hours out of your day. This is a very big commitment and should not be undertaken lightly.

If you have a large house with a large garden and plenty of time to spare, Afghans can be enormous fun. They enjoy playing games with children though occasionally they may seem aloof. Starved of exercise they can become frustrated and neurotic. They are generally non-aggressive dogs and you should have few problems in calling them away from fights. Howling may need Reform School methods to effect a cure (see Chapter 3: "Noisy Dogs").

DELINQUENCY RATING: Low – they do not look for trouble.
HOUSING NEEDS: High – you need a spacious house with a spacious garden.
EXERCISE NEEDS: High – a 30-minute run twice a day.
GROOMING NEEDS: High – a long fine coat, which needs 15 to 20 minutes' brushing every day to prevent unwanted shedding.
FOOD COSTS: Medium to high – one to one and a quarter pounds of food per day.

This is the dog with a fatal combination of delinquent tendencies – the tough guy qualities of the terrier and the killing ability of the hunting hound. It likes nothing better than a good brawl to show its authority over other dogs. Because of its size, it usually wins.

It is the sheer size of the Airedale – about 24 inches tall – that makes them difficult house pets. Most terriers can be picked up and prevented from making trouble, but nobody in his right mind would try to pick up an Airedale.

If you want a dog to keep strangers at bay, this is the ideal candidate. It will bark very loudly, and will not hesitate to use its powerful jaws if given the slightest encouragement. For this reason it must be strictly trained, so that the owner can prevent trouble. Given firm discipline it can make a good house pet.

DELINQUENCY RATING: *High – a born brawler.*
HOUSING NEEDS: *Medium to high – unsuitable for small homes. Height 24 inches.*
EXERCISE NEEDS: *Medium – a 20-minute run, preferably twice a day.*
GROOMING NEEDS: *High – a dense wiry coat, which needs 15 minutes' brushing every day.*
FOOD COSTS: *Medium – three quarters to one pound of food per day.*

This is the Flash Harry's version of the Cocker Spaniel, and is even more trouble. You will need to be fit to cope with the dog's need to exercise. If you skimp on this you could have almost as many delinquency problems as with an English Cocker Spaniel.

But even worse, you will need patience to live with the dog's grooming needs. It has hair everywhere within striking distance of a dirty pavement or puddle. You can expect to spend at least a quarter of an hour every day with a hair brush to keep it in peak condition. If you don't, you will have to put up with hair on your clothes and furniture.

It was bred as an active gundog, and does not like confined spaces. You must have a garden. They are probably calmer than English Cockers, and walk to heel naturally. You should have fewer problems with obedience.

DELINQUENCY RATING: *Medium – slightly less excitable than its English counterpart.*
HOUSING NEEDS: *High – you need a garden even though the dog is a compact 15 inches high.*
EXERCISE NEEDS: *High – half an hour's run morning and evening.*
GROOMING NEEDS: *High – a quarter of an hour with a brush every day and a trip to the beautician every six weeks.*
FOOD COSTS: *Medium to low – 10 to 12 ounces of food a day.*

This is the short back and sides version of the Yorkshire Terrier, and should give you all the advantages of that most popular breed with fewer problems of grooming out the dirt from walks on rainy days.

It is slightly larger than a Yorkie, at about nine inches, but nevertheless is quite compact enough for most modern flats. This is the dog that gets on with the very young and very old equally well, and makes few demands on your time in terms of exercise. Like the Yorkie, many families regard this little dog as an alternative pet to a cat, since it gets most of its exercise running around the house.

It has a reputation for obedience, so you should be able to suppress its terrier temper with your voice. However, should it continue its bad ways, it is small enough to be hoisted clear of trouble, should it take against another dog in the street.

DELINQUENCY RATING:	*Low – friendly and obedient.*
HOUSING NEEDS:	*Low – a couple of rooms is all it needs.*
EXERCISE NEEDS:	*Low – preferably a 10-minute run every day.*
GROOMING NEEDS:	*Medium – five minutes' brushing per day but needs clipping on legs, tail and nose every month.*
FOOD COSTS:	*Low – four to six ounces of food a day.*

First the good news: this is a dog which does not bark. Now the bad news: it squeals instead. You must choose which you find the most endearing or annoying as a sound.

Basenjis are African dogs, and some are alleged to climb like monkeys. Some behave like monkeys too. If it is obedience you are after, do not choose this dog. One day they will be perfectly behaved, the next day you will shout yourself hoarse trying to make them come.

They have a reputation for being food thieves, and some fight among themselves. But by and large, they are not bad-tempered dogs, and their screaming noise has been known to terrify some burglars.

DELINQUENCY RATING:	Medium – obedience is their weak point.
HOUSING NEEDS:	Medium to low – a possibility for a flat dweller even though the dog is 16 inches tall.
EXERCISE NEEDS:	Medium – a 20-minute run preferably twice a day.
GROOMING NEEDS:	Low – two or three minutes a day, but you may choose to put them in a winter coat to keep down hair growth.
FOOD COSTS:	Low – half to three quarters of a pound of food a day.

This looks like a dog desired by a committee. In some ways it was. It is the result of man's desire to have a Bloodhound with short legs. Its very size keeps it from being too delinquent, and to be fair its temperament is extremely appealing. It adapts very well to life in high-rise flats and is a very effective guard-dog. Its bark is Bloodhound-sized, and provided the intruder doesn't catch sight of his titchy opponent, he will almost certainly be deterred.

The Basset Hound's short legs mean that it cannot take much exercise before it becomes tired. Again, this makes it a very suitable pet for town-dwellers. It may show a tendency to stubbornness, but is generally good-natured and self-contained.

DELINQUENCY RATING:	Low – his bark is very much worse than his bite.
HOUSING NEEDS:	Low – very suitable for high-rise apartments. Height 13 to 15 inches.
EXERCISE NEEDS:	Low – a waddler, who will soon tire.
GROOMING NEEDS:	Low – a few minutes' brushing once a week.
FOOD COSTS:	Low – eight ounces to one pound of food daily.

This is a pack dog bred specifically for hunting hare. It is unsuitable as a household pet, especially in homes where there are small children. It is best suited to country homes, where it can get the exercise it needs, and the freedom of the outdoors. In spite of this, thousands of town homes in Britain and America keep Beagles as domestic pets. The dog's size is one of its advantages – it stands only 14 inches high and is therefore less temperamental than other hunting breeds in confined circumstances. But anyone thinking of taking a Beagle on as a pet should make sure they can give it at least two runs of half an hour in the park every day. It is an inexpensive dog to run, but this must be weighed against the amount of effort needed to keep it happy.

DELINQUENCY RATING:	*High – its instinct is to hunt, not to stay indoors. It may become aggressive if not exercised frequently.*
HOUSING NEEDS:	*Low – a small dog, which prefers to be kennelled out of doors. Not suitable for flats.*
EXERCISE NEEDS:	*High – a half-hour run twice daily.*
GROOMING NEEDS:	*Low – short coat needs only five minutes' brushing per day.*
FOOD COSTS:	*Medium to low – half to three quarters of a pound daily.*

This is the dog that most people who buy Old English Sheepdogs really want – if only they knew the difference. It is four to six inches smaller, but generally much more trainable, and a much better house pet. Its coat is very much lighter in weight than that of the Old English Sheepdog, and is therefore much easier to care for. It will not bring as much water into the house on a rainy day, but will still need to be dried down thoroughly. Regular shampooing is necessary – possibly once a month in bad weather.

On the plus side, the dog takes to training very easily, being closely related to the Rough Collie, and is unlikely to jump up at strangers. It is very docile with children provided its coat is not pulled too hard.

Unlike larger dogs, it is possible to accommodate a Bearded Collie in a medium-sized house if there is a park nearby for exercise.

DELINQUENCY RATING:	*Low – generally very friendly and obedient.*
HOUSING NEEDS:	*Medium – a small house with a garden is enough. Height about 20 inches.*
EXERCISE NEEDS:	*Medium – a 20-minute run preferably twice a day.*
GROOMING NEEDS:	*High – most are light in colour and need regular shampooing. Fifteen minutes' brushing daily.*
FOOD COSTS:	*Medium – one to one and a half pounds per day.*

This is a massive dog in every sense of the word, and is happiest in a country setting. It was bred as a sheepdog in Switzerland, and needs a fair amount of exercise to substitute for the work it is designed for.

The dog responds extremely well to training, showing great trust in its owner and being very quick to answer commands. It is good with children, providing it has enough space to keep out of their way from time to time.

The main problems are the dog's appetite and grooming needs. Because it is a working breed it needs a good vitamin-rich diet and at least two pounds of food a day. Its coat is very silky, but to keep its high-sheen appearance you will need to be fairly busy with a hair brush.

DELINQUENCY RATING:	*Low – despite its size it is rarely aggressive.*
HOUSING NEEDS:	*High – definitely unsuitable for high-rise apartments. Prefers medium to large houses. Height about 26 inches.*
EXERCISE NEEDS:	*High – it is used to the mountains of Switzerland; twice-daily runs of 30 minutes are preferable.*
GROOMING NEEDS:	*Low – five minutes of brushing per day.*
FOOD COSTS:	*High – about two pounds of food daily plus added vitamins.*

A large dog more suited to detectives than most family homes. It is renowned for its sense of smell, and if this is what you require, a Basset Hound has many of the same talents while being more manageable.

Bloodhounds may look ferocious but they have very gentle temperaments on the whole, and can be amenable even with young children.

They can be noisy dogs, often howling when their owners leave them behind. Water training, using cups of water or a water pistol, may be necessary to cure them of howling (see Chapter 3: "Noisy Dogs").

They require a great deal of exercise, and are therefore best suited to houses with large gardens, or homes with fields or parkland nearby.

DELINQUENCY RATING:	*Medium – howling is the biggest problem.*
HOUSING NEEDS:	*High – not suitable for small houses or flats. Height about 25 inches.*
EXERCISE NEEDS:	*High – 30 minutes, preferably twice a day.*
GROOMING NEEDS:	*Low – five minutes daily.*
FOOD COSTS:	*High – at least two pounds daily.*

Strictly speaking, Border Collies are working dogs rather than pets. They were bred in the Borders – the sheepfarming area between England and Scotland. Their instinct to herd sheep may cause a few problems, such as an irresistible urge to bite ankles or round up small children. Such dogs need very strict training and the utmost alertness to prevent trouble. However, most Border Collies, if well-chosen, turn out to be agreeable, affectionate pets, with better prospects of successful training than almost any other breed. In obedience competitions, they have dominated for many years.

Be very careful to look at the puppy's parents before buying, to make sure that bad habits are not inbred. For those who do not want the trouble of extra grooming, it is worth choosing a smooth-coated variety. This will cut down the number of unwanted hairs on your furniture.

DELINQUENCY RATING: *Medium to low – very intelligent, very trainable.*
HOUSING NEEDS: *Medium – 16 to 19 inches in height when mature, will fit happily into small houses and ground-floor flats.*
EXERCISE NEEDS: *Medium – lively dogs may need a run of 30 to 45 minutes daily.*
GROOMING NEEDS: *Medium to low – about five minutes a day for smooth-coated dogs, ten minutes for rough-coated dogs.*
FOOD COSTS: *Medium – after maturity no special feeding is needed. About a pound of food daily, including biscuit.*

Elegant it is not. This is a rough, tough, rabbiting and badgering dog designed to go underground and fight it out. These are not the most endearing qualities in a home.

Nevertheless, Border Terriers can make devoted family pets, even though they will never display the affection of other small breeds. You may have problems in the park because this is a dog which hates to back down when confronted by other people's pets. As with most terriers you must be prepared to be very firm. On the whole prevention is the best course, keeping the dog on the lead and calling it to you as soon as trouble appears on the horizon.

Most owners buy these dogs for one purpose – hunting. They are at their best in full flight after rabbits.

DELINQUENCY RATING:	*Medium – a working terrier with fighting spirit.*
HOUSING NEEDS:	*Low – a small dog usually no more than 12 inches in height, which will adapt to high-rise living.*
EXERCISE NEEDS:	*Low – a 10-minute run twice a day.*
GROOMING NEEDS:	*Medium – 10 minutes' brushing a day to keep down stray hairs.*
FOOD COSTS:	*Low – a quarter to a half pound of food a day.*

This dog was bred to kill wolves, and is not the Hollywood starlet it looks. It is not at all suitable for families with small children, because it comes from the wilds of Russia and lacks a sense of humour. These dogs like to be left alone. They have very quick reactions, and can bite without meaning to be aggressive. Their powerful heads and necks are designed to tear the flesh of their victims, and can cause nasty wounds. Responsible owners will find Borzois very obedient, more so than Afghan Hounds. But they cannot expect great displays of affection.

Grooming and exercise will both take up a lot of your time. This is not a dog for the house-proud.

DELINQUENCY RATING: *High – unless well-trained. Will take no teasing.*
HOUSING NEEDS: *High – at around 27 inches in height you need a large house with easy access to open country.*
EXERCISE NEEDS: *High – a 30-minute run twice a day.*
GROOMING NEEDS: *High – 10 to 15 minutes' brushing per day. If kept indoors shedding may be a problem.*
FOOD COSTS: *Medium to high – one to one and a half pounds of food a day.*

These dogs make wonderful family pets, if only you could buy one. There is a waiting list at most British breeders because there are so many difficulties in bringing the puppies into the world alive. Bitches are given Caesarean operations as a rule rather than as an exception. But provided you can wait, a Boston will be a boisterous, cheerful, undemanding companion. The late billionaire Paul Getty kept them – many people think to cheer him up as he sat long-faced surrounded by his vast wealth.

They are excellent playmates for babies; obedient, and have a bark much louder than their size would suggest. Many live on farms as working cattle dogs.

In addition, they make very small demands in terms of exercise and grooming, and are quite happy to live in flats.

DELINQUENCY RATING:	*Low – but watch out for the terrier in their soul.*
HOUSING NEEDS:	*Low – even high-rise living will do. Height around 15 inches.*
EXERCISE NEEDS:	*Low – a 10-minute run, preferably twice a day.*
GROOMING NEEDS:	*Low – they don't even moult.*
FOOD COSTS:	*Medium to low – three quarters to one and a quarter pounds of food per day.*

Boxers look as if they are ready for a fight, but their faces are much more aggressive than their temperament. However, a great many Boxers do have delinquency problems because their owners totally underestimate their needs. These are very boisterous dogs, which need a great deal of exercise. They enjoy running flat out, and if denied this release of energy may become aggressive.

They have a tendency to dribble from the mouth, which may cause annoyance around the house. Parents with young children may not feel it desirable to let such a pet get too close to their children's faces for reasons of hygiene. However, Boxers are generally very friendly to children, especially if they are given enough house room. Some may be aggressive to dogs, while friendly to humans.

DELINQUENCY RATING:	High – a powerful, muscular dog, which needs more room than most families have to offer.
HOUSING NEEDS:	High – very active dogs needing lots of house room. Height about 24 inches.
EXERCISE NEEDS:	High – bred as a hunting dog and sheepdog – needs at least 30 minutes of free running, preferably twice daily.
GROOMING NEEDS:	Low – a quick brush twice a week.
FOOD COSTS:	High to medium – needs one and a half to two pounds of meat and biscuit per day.

Not as good a bet as a Bearded Collie, but a very attractive dog for those who like large cuddly pets.

Briards are similar in size to the Old English Sheepdog and are generally less excitable. Occasionally they can be introverted and need a lot of socialising to bring them out.

They are used as sheepdogs in their native France, but they are not as easy to train as Border Collies. With little effort, however, you should have an obedient, non-aggressive family pet on your hands.

Grooming needs are less than those of an Old English Sheepdog, but those dogs with a dense undercoat can cause you quite a few problems.

DELINQUENCY RATING:	*Low – good with children.*
HOUSING NEEDS:	*Medium to high – they can adapt to very small houses. Height 25 inches.*
EXERCISE NEEDS:	*Medium – a 20-minute run twice a day.*
GROOMING NEEDS:	*Medium – 10 minutes' brushing a day.*
FOOD COSTS:	*High – one and a quarter to three pounds of food a day depending on size and exercise.*

British Bulldogs are world-renowned for their stubbornness. Almost everything people say is true. However, ferocious as this dog looks, it has quite a sweet temper, and most will play happily with children. Just below the surface is a breeding history as a fighting dog, a dog that was meant to bait bulls. In exceptional cases this old ferocity can surface, and present the owner with a thoroughly objectionable pet. The dog's squat build means that it does not want much exercise. But don't let this fool you into thinking that the dog is suitable for granny in her tiny high-rise flat. For a start, it weighs over 50 pounds, and is not the sort of dog you can tuck under your arm in the lift. One plus point: Bulldogs rarely bark.

DELINQUENCY RATING:	Medium – check the parents for signs of ferocity.
HOUSING NEEDS:	Medium – not suitable for very small houses.
EXERCISE NEEDS:	Low – a 10-minute run, preferably twice a day.
GROOMING NEEDS:	Low – a couple of minutes' brushing every day.
FOOD COSTS:	Medium – a pound and a quarter to a pound and a half a day.

This massive animal is one of the best guard-dogs in the world. It will protect the home against all-comers, but can be easily controlled. Its instinct is not to chase and bite, but to repel. However, its sheer size – weighing in at well over a hundred pounds and standing 25 inches tall – can cause problems if the dog turns out to be nervous through breeding faults.

Running costs are high because the dog has such a large appetite. You can expect it to eat two and a half pounds of food a day.

Grooming needs are very low, and the dog does not make much mess in rainy weather. However, there is a tendency to drool, something which won't appeal to families with young children, who may come in close contact with the dog's face.

DELINQUENCY RATING:	*High – it may severely injure a visitor it mistakes for an intruder.*
HOUSING NEEDS:	*High – suitable for large homes with gardens.*
EXERCISE NEEDS:	*Medium – a 20-minute run, preferably twice a day.*
GROOMING NEEDS:	*Low – two minutes of brushing per day.*
FOOD COSTS:	*High – two and a half pounds of food per day.*

Thankfully, Bull Terriers are no longer the vicious companions to thugs like Bill Sykes, the psychopath immortalised in Charles Dickens' *Oliver Twist*. By careful breeding, the dog's courage has been retained, while its bully-boy qualities have been suppressed.

Bull Terriers will not go looking for a fight, but if another dog starts trouble you will have difficulty calling it off. It does not like to be beaten. For this reason you must be careful to anticipate trouble and train the dog to obey the basic commands without hesitation.

Its striking appearance with its bulbous nose makes it appealing to many people who want an imposing guard-dog as well as an unusual pet. Bull Terriers make surprisingly good house pets, with few signs of temperamental tantrums. But they will not tolerate teasing by children.

DELINQUENCY RATING:	*High – most owners cannot control them.*
HOUSING NEEDS:	*Medium – a muscular dog standing about 16 inches high. Unsuitable for small homes.*
EXERCISE NEEDS:	*Medium – a 20-minute run, preferably twice a day.*
GROOMING NEEDS:	*Low – five minutes' brushing per day.*
FOOD COSTS:	*Medium – three quarters of a pound to one pound of food per day.*

One of the most popular terriers in Britain, so presumably the sheer number of owners prove how lovable Cairns are generally thought to be. However, some Cairns have been known to be snappy with strangers. Most merely keep their distance, only responding to strangers once they have had time to get used to them. Only a few show genuine aggression, but it is a good idea to assess the temperament of the puppy's parents before buying.

Cairn Terriers respond well to obedience training, but once they have found that they can bark, they may be difficult to quieten down. You may have to work hard at socialising the dog with children to prevent incidents of aggression. Some Cairns are snappy with other dogs, and strict training is necessary to keep them under control.

DELINQUENCY RATING:	*Medium – very trainable, but a minority are snappy with strangers, children and other dogs.*
HOUSING NEEDS:	*Low – adults grow to around 10 inches tall, and are very self-contained.*
EXERCISE NEEDS:	*Low – about 10 minutes once or twice a day.*
GROOMING NEEDS:	*Low – wiry coat needs three or four minutes' brushing per day.*
FOOD COSTS:	*Low – six to eight ounces of food per day.*

The almost perfect pet, friendly, responsive to training and trustworthy with children. Its name comes from the days when it was the favourite dog of King Charles the Second of England. The modern version of the dog is almost identical in size and temperament to the original – a breed which became unfashionable and nearly died out in the nineteenth century. Its looks are those of an ancient hunting spaniel, but its temperament is very much more suited to the modern home. It is always happy to welcome visitors; it will even give you its chair – in the hope that you will let it share its company, side by side.

It is a small dog – only about 12 inches high, and is therefore ideal for anyone with limited space and limited time for exercise. Most dogs are happy with a ten-minute run, preferably twice a day.

DELINQUENCY RATING:	Low – very responsive to training; docile and spirited.
HOUSING NEEDS:	Low – fits snugly into an armchair.
EXERCISE NEEDS:	Low – can run surprisingly fast, but will be happy with a 10-minute run.
GROOMING NEEDS:	Medium – easily groomed but must be kept tidy around its throat feather. About five minutes daily.
FOOD COSTS:	Low – six to eight ounces daily including biscuit.

This is the smallest breed in the world, weighing around four pounds when fully grown and standing only five or six inches high. For this very reason it is ideally suited to small-scale accommodation, and will exercise itself around the home, with only the minimum of outdoor exercise being needed. It is ideal both for the elderly and for families with young children. It is full of character, alert, affectionate and easily trained. The long-coated variety needs about five minutes of grooming every day. The short-coated variety can be groomed in less than a minute using a suede glove.

It responds to training very well, and does not have a reputation for aggression.

DELINQUENCY RATING: *Low – it is small and friendly.*
HOUSING NEEDS: *Low – a caravan is amply big enough.*
EXERCISE NEEDS: *Low – 10 minutes a day, if you have time.*
GROOMING NEEDS: *Low – the smooth-coated variety needs virtually none.*
FOOD COSTS: *Low – two to three ounces per day.*

They look like lions, and if an intruder tries to break into your home they can fight like lions. This is not the best-behaved dog you would ever wish to meet, but if you are tough in your training you might make it into a manageable pet.

You may well have problems getting a chow to come when it is called, and you can forget about asking the dog to retrieve. Very few will oblige. They have a reputation for being intolerant of boisterous children. They are not the most outgoing of dogs, and a pull on their lion's mane might well be met by a nip on the hand.

Grooming is not as formidable as it looks in terms of time spent. You will have to use a wire brush for best results.

DELINQUENCY RATING:	*Medium – a bit touchy.*
HOUSING NEEDS:	*Medium – a smaller house and garden will do. Height 18 inches.*
EXERCISE NEEDS:	*Medium – a 20-minute run, preferably twice a day.*
GROOMING NEEDS:	*Medium – five to 10 minutes' brushing every day.*
FOOD COSTS:	*Low – half to three quarters of a pound of food a day.*

This dog is very much more popular than its near relative the English Springer Spaniel, though it is far more delinquent. It is an excitable animal, and so headstrong that training may prove very time-consuming. Anyone torn between the looks of these two kinds of spaniels should choose the more placid English Springer variety.

You'll have to spend time to keep its silky coat in trim, especially the feathering on the chest and legs.

It needs a lot of exercise to keep its excitability in check, and for this reason is unsuitable for anyone without a garden. For parents with young children the dog may prove too much of a handful, since it will react eagerly to the children's desire to play, and may be difficult to bring under control when mealtimes or outings are due.

DELINQUENCY RATING:	*Medium to high — excitable and headstrong.*
HOUSING NEEDS:	*High — a garden is desirable, even though the dog is only 16 inches high.*
EXERCISE NEEDS:	*High — as much as possible, preferably half an hour's run twice a day.*
GROOMING NEEDS:	*Medium — 10 minutes daily and twice-yearly trimming.*
FOOD COSTS:	*Low — three quarters of a pound of food daily.*

This is a highly obedient dog, bred first as a sheepdog in the Scottish Highlands. It is very successful in obedience competitions because of its quickness of mind and alertness. These qualities are very desirable in busy homes, where a dog of this size must know its place.

Rough Collies are excellent with small children, tolerant of a fair amount of rough and tumble without losing their tempers, and big enough not to be pushed around. They also make good guard-dogs, having big voices without unwanted aggression. They are more interested in defence than attack. As with all sheepdogs you may have problems with the dog's instinct to round animals up – the animals may well be your neighbour's children. A rewarding pet.

DELINQUENCY RATING: *Low – the star of the "Lassie" films for good reason.*
HOUSING NEEDS: *High – a large, energetic dog, which would not be at home in smaller houses or flats. Height 22 inches.*
EXERCISE NEEDS: *High – a 30-minute run twice a day.*
GROOMING NEEDS: *High – the dog's long mane needs a lot of attention to keep down stray hairs on furniture and clothing. At least 15 minutes' brushing every day.*
FOOD COSTS: *Medium – one to one and a half pounds of food a day.*

This is the dog with the royal seal of approval. You could be forgiven for thinking that its connections with the British royal family have given it ideas above its station. Some Corgis can be quite snappy, and it is worth investigating their family trees to make sure that the puppy does not turn out to be an ankle-biter like mum or dad.

Given early training, most Corgis turn out to be friendly and obedient family pets which make few demands in terms of exercise or grooming. They are suitable for flat-dwellers, and because of their low feeding costs are ideal for the elderly, who may not have much money to spare.

For those who like to take the dog for an occasional long walk, the Corgi is capable of a good gallop, despite its short legs. It was originally a cattle dog hence the tendency to chase and bite ankles.

DELINQUENCY RATING: Medium – watch your ankles.
HOUSING NEEDS: Low – you do not need a palace, a bedsitter will do. Height about 11 inches.
EXERCISE NEEDS: Low – a 10-minute run, preferably twice a day.
GROOMING NEEDS: Low – a thick short coat, which needs about five minutes' brushing a day.
FOOD COSTS: Low to medium – three quarters of a pound a day.

Its looks are improbable, but its temperament is entirely suited to town life. It is quiet, obedient and an excellent watch-dog.

Its secret is that it doesn't have extremes of temperament, and is generally very easy to train. It is affectionate, without developing the dependence on its owner exhibited by other small dogs.

Because of its short legs it does not need much exercise. It is equally at home in an apartment as in a house, though it appreciates open ground – it was bred as a rabbiting dog and loves to root around in wild places. The smooth-haired variety has earned the breed its nickname of "sausage dog".

But there are long- and wire-haired varieties as well. None of them requires much grooming.

DELINQUENCY RATING:	*Low – a small dog with a friendly disposition.*
HOUSING NEEDS:	*Low – suitable for high-rise apartments. Height around 12 inches.*
EXERCISE NEEDS:	*Low – a 10-minute run daily.*
GROOMING NEEDS:	*Low – even the long-haired variety needs only five minutes' grooming daily.*
FOOD COSTS:	*Low – half a pound of food per day.*

Dalmatians make wonderful pets for families with small children and modest accommodation. You can expect a lot of attention when you take the dog for a walk, but since it is such a friendly animal, the interest of strangers should not prove a problem.

This is a very friendly dog around the home. It will show great trust and affection to friends and family, while being an effective watch-dog. It is easy to train, and you should have few problems with getting it to come when called.

Their dense, smooth, spotted coat needs next to no grooming, and is not prone to shedding hair, something which makes it attractive to house-proud owners.

"Spotted Dick" is an agile and fast running dog and prefers long runs every day. However, it will make do with moderate amounts of exercise during the week, provided it can have a good gallop at weekends.

DELINQUENCY RATING:	*Low – it didn't star in the Walt Disney film for no reason.*
HOUSING NEEDS:	*Medium – it can make do with a small house and garden. Height 20 inches.*
EXERCISE NEEDS:	*Medium – a 20-minute run preferably twice a day.*
GROOMING NEEDS:	*Low – two minutes' brushing every day.*
FOOD COSTS:	*Medium – one to one and a quarter pounds of food per day.*

This is a bit of a traitor to the terrier clan – it has a distinctly soft streak. Some owners claim it is more hound-like in temperament in that it refuses to be snappy in the face of quite strong provocation. It is said to adore games of hide and seek with children, but this is rarely put to the test since so few of the breed are available for sale.

It is a dog which will fight for the affection of each member of the family in turn. Its terrier-like qualities are mostly displayed towards other dogs. It will often chase other dogs away in the park, before scurrying back to its owner. They can be greedy dogs and must be limited to small meals to prevent them putting on weight.

Exercise needs are relatively small, making them potentially good pets for the elderly. Grooming is comparatively easy but because they are double-coated, dead hair should be teased out by hand. Clipping alters the texture of its silken hair.

DELINQUENCY RATING: *Low – very placid for a terrier.*
HOUSING NEEDS: *Low – suitable for high-rise homes. Height around 10 inches.*
EXERCISE NEEDS: *Low – a 10-minute run twice a day.*
GROOMING NEEDS: *Low to medium – five to 10 minutes a day.*
FOOD COSTS: *Low – half a pound of food per day.*

This is a friendly scruff of a dog, despite its rather ferocious appearance. It is very good with young children and takes quite a bit of teasing before it tires. Its size should not rule it out for even modest-sized homes. This is not the best guard-dog ever devised. It is so friendly that it is hard to imagine that it would consider a burglar capable of doing any harm. You must hope that its size – 28 inches tall on average – will frighten any intruder off.

They are not expensive dogs to run, considering their size, and need grooming only once a week. Any more would lose them their slept-in look.

DELINQUENCY RATING:	*Low – if anything they are too nice.*
HOUSING NEEDS:	*Medium – big dogs that make small space demands.*
EXERCISE NEEDS:	*High – a 30-minute run twice a day.*
GROOMING NEEDS:	*Low – only needs brushing for half an hour once a week.*
FOOD COSTS:	*Medium – a pound and a quarter of food a day.*

A superb guard-dog used by many police forces throughout the world for crowd control. It is a tall, powerful dog, which needs firm handling to make sure its aggressive tendencies do not get out of order. The breed is inclined to be excitable, and no attempt to encourage its aggressiveness should be made. Few owners would be able to control such aggression once it had got out of hand.

It is a dog which needs a great deal of exercise and should not be considered by anyone living in a home without a garden. High-rise apartments are likely to bring out the worst side of its nature.

Dobermanns are not the most ideal pets for families with small children. They tend to respond most to one person, rather than crave affection from the whole family.

DELINQUENCY RATING:	*High – a large dog which often falls into the wrong hands. Needs careful training.*
HOUSING NEEDS:	*High – this is a high-energy dog with a touch of terrier in its breeding. Height around 25 inches. Garden highly desirable.*
EXERCISE NEEDS:	*High – a half-hour run twice a day, preferably on open ground.*
GROOMING NEEDS:	*Low – very short smooth coat needs virtually no attention.*
FOOD COSTS:	*High – two pounds of food daily.*

This is more of a working dog than a pet. It was bred as a gundog, and is at its best racing towards game in the open fields.

Unlike the Irish Setter, however, this is a trainable dog which can make a good family pet. But it needs a large home with a garden and plenty of access to open spaces if it is to be really happy.

Its temperament is gentle and affectionate, and it will tolerate small children up to a point. You must be sure that you can give the dog the time it needs for exercise, otherwise its energy may make it neurotic. Grooming must also be considered. The considerable feathering on the chest, tail, legs and ears means about 15 minutes of brushing daily.

DELINQUENCY RATING:	*Medium to low – a very placid dog for its size.*
HOUSING NEEDS:	*High – a garden is preferable. Unsuitable for small houses or flats. Height about 25 inches.*
EXERCISE NEEDS:	*High – a good half-hour run twice daily in open country.*
GROOMING NEEDS:	*Medium to high – 15 minutes' brushing per day.*
FOOD COSTS:	*Medium – one to one and a half pounds of food a day.*

This is an ideal pet for somebody who lives in a medium-sized home. Springer Spaniels are friendly, happy and excellent with children. Another big plus point is their comparative lack of bark – something that makes them welcome neighbours to people who prefer dogs to be seen and not heard.

Even though they have been bred as gundogs, they will adapt very easily to town life, needing relatively little exercise.

The long glossy coat needs quite a bit of grooming to keep it in shape. This will also reduce the amount of clipping necessary. It should need a trip to the hairdresser's twice a year on average.

DELINQUENCY RATING: *Low – much less temperamental than the Cocker Spaniel.*
HOUSING NEEDS: *Medium to large – unsuitable for life in flats. Height about 20 inches.*
EXERCISE NEEDS: *Medium – very adaptable – loves to run free but will adapt to as little as 20 minutes' exercise once a day.*
GROOMING NEEDS: *Medium to high – 10 minutes' brushing per day; clipping every six months.*
FOOD COSTS: *Medium to low – half to three quarters of a pound of food a day.*

This is a ratter with a strong domestic streak. It is closely related to the much larger Manchester Terrier, and has inherited its ability to catch rats and destroy them with a flick of its head. If it is kennelled with other English Toy Terriers, fights can develop, and it has been known for two dogs to gang up and kill a third.

By themselves, however, they are very affectionate dogs, happy to sit on their owner's lap. They are very quick in their movements and may occasionally appear nervous.

With children they will behave consistently. If they don't like being played with one day they will not like being played with the next. Yet some are tolerant of boisterous children.

Their size makes them suitable for flats, and elderly people will not find their exercise needs too demanding.

DELINQUENCY RATING: *Low – but beware of other dogs in the park.*
HOUSING NEEDS: *Low – quite happy in the smallest of homes standing only six to 12 inches tall.*
EXERCISE NEEDS: *Low – a 10-minute run, preferably twice a day.*
GROOMING NEEDS: *Low – virtually non-existent – only a couple of minutes a day.*
FOOD COSTS: *Low – but proportionately high for its size at up to half a pound of food per day.*

Until recently this was the most popular terrier around, and it is not difficult to see why. It has many saving graces to counteract its instincts to show aggression, especially to other dogs.

Fox Terriers seem more alive than most dogs. They are always alert, on the look-out for danger. This makes them good watch-dogs; you will rarely have a visitor arrive unannounced. You may have to work at stopping the dog barking.

Since most people choose the wire-haired variety for its craggy looks, grooming is a factor which must be taken into account when you add up the time you have each week for your dog. To keep the desired bushiness in the leg and whisker hair may take as much as 20 minutes of daily brushing because the dog's coat is so harsh and thick.

Fox Terriers make good family pets if they are carefully trained, and their size, at 14 to 15 inches tall, makes them suitable for most homes with small gardens.

DELINQUENCY RATING:	Medium – they may fight with other dogs.
HOUSING NEEDS:	Medium – not suitable for high-rise apartments.
EXERCISE NEEDS:	Medium – a 20-minute run twice daily.
GROOMING NEEDS:	High – 20 minutes' brushing daily for the wire-haired variety, two or three minutes for the smooth-haired variety.
FOOD COSTS:	Medium to low – three quarters of a pound of food per day.

This is the Nice Guy's Bulldog. It's half the weight of the British Bulldog, and twice as likeable. If one of these dogs bites you, you probably deserve it.

They are too boisterous for flats, and have a tendency to jump all over your furniture. The few that have gone in for serious obedience training have made heavy weather of it. You have to really shout to get through to them at all.

They are not a barking dog, except when their territory is being invaded. Once the coast is clear, they will fall silent again.

They do not like being kennelled out of doors. They genuinely seek the company of human beings.

DELINQUENCY RATING: *Low to medium – but watch your ornaments around the house.*
HOUSING NEEDS: *Low – but their high energy makes them difficult in flats. Height about 15 inches.*
EXERCISE NEEDS: *Low – a 10-minute run, preferably twice a day.*
GROOMING NEEDS: *Low – two or three minutes' brushing once or twice a week.*
FOOD COSTS: *Medium – one and a half pounds of food a day.*

By far the most popular dog in Britain, and, because of its size, by far the most badly treated. This is not a dog suited to high-rise flats or small houses, yet thousands of them have to suffer such conditions because their owners want a dog to frighten strangers away. Unlike other dogs, their aggression is often encouraged by owners. This is a most dangerous practice, since, unlike policemen, pet owners rarely have any real control over their pets, and cannot command the dog to stop its aggression.

However, provided you have the space and the time for a German Shepherd Dog, this can be the most wonderful pet. It is intelligent, very responsive to training, and very affectionate and loyal to the family. This loyalty can make the dog unfriendly to strangers and it is therefore doubly necessary to make sure that the dog will sit, stay and come on command.

DELINQUENCY RATING:	*High – because of its size, it needs a very sensible owner.*
HOUSING NEEDS:	*High – dogs are around 25 inches tall. Not suitable for high-rise flats or small houses.*
EXERCISE NEEDS:	*High – ideally two half-hour runs per day.*
GROOMING NEEDS:	*Low to medium – long-coated dogs need about five or six minutes' grooming every day; short-coated dogs need three to five.*
FOOD COSTS:	*High – rapid growth in puppies. Adults need two pounds daily.*

This is a difficult dog for life in the suburbs. It is bred for hunting, and if you let it out in an unfenced garden, it will be over the hills and far away and will develop sudden deafness when you call.

These are not the most intelligent of dogs, and need a strong-willed owner to get any obedience lesson understood. In the hunting field, they are good all-rounders, and this could cause you problems if your daily walk takes you anywhere near rabbits, chickens or sheep. A full-blooded chase will be difficult to prevent.

In the house they are faithful, friendly and generally tolerant of small children.

DELINQUENCY RATING: *Medium – you need a loud voice to get them to obey.*
HOUSING NEEDS: *Medium to high – quite a large dog at about 23 inches tall, your garden needs to be well fenced.*
EXERCISE NEEDS: *High – a 30-minute run, preferably twice a day.*
GROOMING NEEDS: *Low – two to five minutes' brushing a day, with rubber comb.*
FOOD COSTS: *Medium – one and a half pounds of food a day.*

This is not a dog for someone with a nine to five job. By the time you return home, half your three-piece suite may be in tatters. Giant Schnauzers are big dogs, which get bored easily.

It makes an excellent guard-dog, however. Its white teeth against its jet-black beard are a terrifying sight. Add to this its strong deep bark, and you should not be troubled by intruders.

They can be trained to quite a high degree, a testament to their shepherding background, but they will never win first prize for quickness of response. You should have few problems with aggression.

In the home, they do not shed their coats like a Collie, but they need people around them at all times to keep them occupied. Otherwise, they may look to the furniture for amusement, and chew anything in sight.

DELINQUENCY RATING: Medium – they need company.
HOUSING NEEDS: Medium – too big for flats at around 26 inches tall.
EXERCISE NEEDS: Medium – a 20-minute run twice a day.
GROOMING NEEDS: Medium – Only two to three minutes' brushing a day but keep the beard clean after feeding.
FOOD COSTS: High – two to two and a half pounds of food a day.

This is usually as friendly a dog as it looks, a warm, solid, outgoing reliable sort of creature. Only rarely does a bad-tempered specimen crop up, and it is worth taking a good look at the puppy's parents to make sure that it is not the exception.

They require more exercise and grooming than most people bargain for, but that is no great obstacle. In return for a couple of half-hour runs every day the dog will give endless loyalty and affection. It tolerates young children well, and is generally very obedient.

They were bred as gundogs as their name implies, and their instinct is to retrieve. Be very careful not to throw sticks in the park, as some dogs have died through splinters lodging in their throat. Use a rubber ring instead.

DELINQUENCY RATING:	*Medium to low – only the exceptional dog is nasty.*
HOUSING NEEDS:	*Medium to high – they were bred as country dogs and prefer houses with gardens. Height: around 22 inches.*
EXERCISE NEEDS:	*High – a 30-minute run twice a day.*
GROOMING NEEDS:	*Medium to high – the dog's coat sheds water easily but the feathering on the chest and tail will need about 15 minutes' brushing a day.*
FOOD COSTS:	*Medium – one to one and a half pounds daily.*

If you do not value your ornaments, and you have a house with acres of space, this might be the dog for you. But unless you are considering using the dog for field trials or as a gundog, you should probably let your head rule your heart and avoid this dog. They have boundless energy and they are very large for most homes. Although their temperament is friendly, they are like bulls in china shops, knocking over everything and everyone in sight.

They need a great deal of exercise every day to work off their energy and thrive best in country settings, especially if there is access to large fields.

DELINQUENCY RATING: *High – an energetic working dog unsuitable for town life.*
HOUSING NEEDS: *High – needs open fields. Height is 24–27 inches.*
EXERCISE NEEDS: *High – half an hour of good running twice a day.*
GROOMING NEEDS: *Medium to high – 10 to 15 minutes a day.*
FOOD COSTS: *High – a large dog needing two pounds of food daily.*

A status dog that often becomes delinquent because pride outstrips it's owner's ability to care for the animal's great needs. This is a massive dog standing nearly 30 inches tall and needing at least an hour's exercise every day. Yet often in towns it is confined to small houses with virtually no garden, and its only exercise is a stroll to the shops and an occasional weekend run. All this can make some Great Danes neurotic.

Considering their size, Great Danes are very affectionate dogs, suitable for homes with small children. They are easy to train, but this must be done at an early age, when they are still small enough to be controllable. Otherwise, there is the danger that they may pull their owners or their owner's children into the path of traffic while out walking.

Running costs are high, and the dog should really only be considered by those with large amounts of disposable income and time.

DELINQUENCY RATING: *Medium – rarely aggressive but can be neurotic if denied space.*
HOUSING NEEDS: *High – only larger homes with gardens are suitable.*
EXERCISE NEEDS: *High – it needs a good run in a park for half an hour twice daily.*
GROOMING NEEDS: *Low – a few minutes a week.*
FOOD COSTS: *High – two to two and a half pounds daily.*

Greyhounds need to run, not just occasionally but each and every day. If you are not prepared to set aside at least an hour each day, do not buy one.

If confined at home for days on end, greyhounds may become snappy. They are bred to chase and kill small game and may have a tendency towards aggression in domestic situations. It is important to socialise the dogs as much as possible to make them more friendly to strangers. In the best of circumstances they are not very affectionate dogs, and for this reason they are not the best pets for families with small children. They will play when they want to and not when the child wants them to. In the park, they need to stretch out in a good long run. Since they can reach speeds of over 40 miles per hour you must be sure they will come when they are called. Otherwise, you may be in trouble if they decide to chase someone else's small pet.

DELINQUENCY RATING:	Medium – neurotic if not exercised.
HOUSING NEEDS:	High – a very tall dog, around 28 inches in height, which needs spacious rooms in a house near a park.
EXERCISE NEEDS:	High – a 30-minute run, twice a day.
GROOMING NEEDS:	Low – five minutes' brushing per day.
FOOD COSTS:	High – one and a half pounds of food a day.

This is a clever little dog, which is better than a burglar alarm at sensing trouble outside. It is ideal for old people who are getting hard of hearing because it will let them know whenever anyone is at the door. It will also give as much affection as it gets.

As with many small dogs, Griffons are quite dependent on their owners, and cannot be left alone too long without beginning to fret. But since they are small enough to put in a shopping bag, you can probably take them with you no matter where you go. They are not the kind of dog to make themselves a nuisance in public places by snapping and barking.

They are playful dogs, but you should warn young children not to be too rough with them. They can be hurt easily. Exercise is no problem if you have a garden. You will not have to take them out for walks at all.

DELINQUENCY RATING:	Low – a little over-dependent.
HOUSING NEEDS:	Low – the dog is only nine inches tall.
EXERCISE NEEDS:	Low – a 10-minute walk every day.
GROOMING NEEDS:	Low – two or three minutes' brushing every day, clip eyebrows regularly.
FOOD COSTS:	Low – around six ounces of food a day.

This is very closely related to the Tervueren, but is more favoured for police work because of its deep black colour – very good for showing off the teeth.

Think of this as an alternative to a German Shepherd Dog. If anything, it has a slightly sweeter nature, but there's little to choose between the two in terms of trainability, or ability to defend its owner's territory. This is not a dog to be treated casually. It is slightly taller than a German Shepherd Dog, and could do as much damage in the wrong hands. If you are looking for a guard-dog, this could be a good choice.

If you are prepared to put in the time for training, a Groenendael can make an affectionate family pet. It will take to children well, but you must be prepared to sacrifice time at the beginning and end of every day for exercise.

DELINQUENCY RATING: *Medium to high – a powerful dog, lethal in the wrong hands.*
HOUSING NEEDS: *High – medium to large house only. Height 24 inches.*
EXERCISE NEEDS: *High – a half-hour run morning and evening.*
GROOMING NEEDS: *High – 15 minutes' brushing daily.*
FOOD COSTS: *Medium – one and a quarter pounds of food a day.*

This is an Irish joke played on unsuspecting owners throughout the world. The Irish Setter's film star good looks and silken red hair deceive many people into thinking that their relationship with the dog will be a never-ending romance. Nothing could be further from the truth.

This is one of the daftest dogs around. It has a friendly temperament, showing not the slightest sign of aggression, but it is scatter-brained and never knows when to stop.

You can expect it to try to sit on visitors' knees, to stand on its hind legs and constantly try to lick your face, to be on the move all the time, in the quest for more affection.

Training can be time-consuming. The most difficult lesson is teaching an Irish Setter to come when it is called. In large parks you may not see the dog again for 20 minutes.

DELINQUENCY RATING:	*High – a large dog with a small brain.*
HOUSING NEEDS:	*High – they are 24 inches tall and need a garden if they are not going to drive you mad.*
EXERCISE NEEDS:	*High – it was bred as a gundog, and likes long country runs, at least one 30-minute gallop a day.*
GROOMING NEEDS:	*Medium to high – 15 minutes a day.*
FOOD COSTS:	*High – one and three quarter pounds a day.*

There is more than a touch of the Airedale Terrier about this dog, especially in its fighting spirit. Woe betide any dog you pass in the park when it is off the lead.

It is quite a bit smaller than the Airedale, but still big for a terrier, and you will have considerable problems keeping it under control when it takes a dislike to another dog. They make excellent guard-dogs when you are away, but may annoy your neighbours by their inability to know when to stop barking.

Training needs a very firm hand indeed, if this is to make anything like a good housedog. It might be easier on your nerves if you have a large garden, because the dogs need to burn off a lot of energy every day, and can be quite a nuisance in flats. Nevertheless, many owners successfully keep them in high-rise apartments.

DELINQUENCY RATING: High – they never back down from a fight.
HOUSING NEEDS: Medium – they are about 18 inches tall and a garden is preferable.
EXERCISE NEEDS: Medium – a 20-minute run twice a day.
GROOMING NEEDS: Low – a hard wiry coat, which does not shed hair if stripped twice a year. Brush two to three minutes daily.
FOOD COSTS: Medium – three quarters to a pound of food a day.

They look like poodles, and have many of their near relatives' virtues. They do not moult, and their springy hair should not affect anyone who has an allergy to dog hair. In addition they are well-behaved, if a little boisterous.

This is not a dog for the elderly, because it will not understand that it should not pull them along. But it is comparatively easy to train, and has no real problems of aggression.

It has been bred to retrieve game in water, and likes nothing better than a swim. It is reputed to be so gentle with its mouth that it can lift an egg to shore without breaking it.

It is a good dog with children, and should not bark at your friends, only at strangers. Bad breeding has recently left a strain which can be snappy. Check the parents of any puppy you buy.

DELINQUENCY RATING:	*Low – but beware snappy strain.*
HOUSING NEEDS:	*Medium – needs access to open space. Height around 22 inches.*
EXERCISE NEEDS:	*Medium – a 20-minute run twice a day.*
GROOMING NEEDS:	*High – half an hour's brushing twice or three times a week, and clipping every six weeks.*
FOOD COSTS:	*Medium – about one and a half pounds of food daily.*

This is the tallest breed in the world at around 30 inches on average. But it is as soft and gentle a family pet as anyone could wish for. Unfortunately, many families take them on as a status symbol and find they cannot cope. In Britain a rescue service had to be set up by breeders for dogs that had become too much of a handful for their owners.

An Irish Wolfhound is one of the least aggressive dogs around, in spite of its forbidding appearance. Small children can ride on its back with no problem. But it needs a lot of exercise, and is quite expensive to run. It should not be taken on lightly, and owners should have very large gardens or access to nearby open space.

As with many hounds, you may have howling and barking problems. In this case the bigger the dog the louder the bark.

DELINQUENCY RATING: Low – sweet-natured.
HOUSING NEEDS: High – as you would expect with the world's tallest dog.
EXERCISE NEEDS: High – a half-hour run twice a day in open country.
GROOMING NEEDS: Low – five minutes' brushing every day.
FOOD COSTS: High – two and a half pounds of food a day.

This is a housedog par excellence, and you can match the size of dog to your home. The largest are as big as Cavalier King Charles Spaniels, standing around 11 inches tall. The smallest may be only seven inches tall.

They have much in common with Pekingese, though they do not have a reputation for being yappy, and are suitable for the elderly, with limited accommodation. They are not suitable for families with boisterous young children, being far too delicate to stand up to rough play.

They are not renowned for their obedience, and will try to get away with as much as they can.

Grooming takes time, but by no means as much as other oriental breeds.

DELINQUENCY RATING:	*Low – but rather cheeky.*
HOUSING NEEDS:	*Low – bred for Japanese-scale living.*
EXERCISE NEEDS:	*Low – a 10 to 20-minute walk every day.*
GROOMING NEEDS:	*Medium – five to 10 minutes' brushing every day.*
FOOD COSTS:	*Medium to low – between eight ounces and one pound of food a day depending on size.*

These elegant little dogs are seen on verandas outside thousands of Japanese homes. Their purpose is both decorative and functional. They will bark very loudly at any stranger who crosses the threshold.

Though rare in Britain, they are equally suited to small-scale living in the west. Their white coat is not as impractical as it looks, because it is weather-resistant, and sheds water. Unlike other long-haired dogs it will not stain rugs when it has come in from the wet.

It needs a firm owner to train it well, as it tends to be a little self-willed. It needs introducing gently to small children, and does not like teasing.

Its barking may annoy. Males are extremely noisy every time the telephone rings.

DELINQUENCY RATING: *Low – a little yappy.*
HOUSING NEEDS: *Low – no need for a garden. Height around 11 inches.*
EXERCISE NEEDS: *Low – a 10-minute walk, preferably twice a day.*
GROOMING NEEDS: *Medium to high – 10 minutes' brushing every day.*
FOOD COSTS: *Low – eight or nine ounces of food per day.*

This is a real fiery Celt of a dog with one soft and endearing characteristic – its woolly coat. It is covered in woollen curls, which make it ideal for families with allergies to dog hair. It cuts down the housework too because it does not shed its wool. It has virtually no odour, something which will please those who have non dog-loving friends. Kerry Blues can be a little grumpy with other dogs, a characteristic typical of its terrier blood. But it is quite easily trained and may demonstrate considerable affection.

Grooming is a problem. Its magnificent coat, prized throughout its native Ireland, especially in its dark blue form, takes a lot of caring for. It needs 20 minutes' brushing every day and clipping twice a year. It is a medium-sized dog, but suits houses rather than flats, largely because of its high spirits and relatively high exercise needs.

DELINQUENCY RATING:	*Medium – avoid other dogs in the park.*
HOUSING NEEDS:	*Medium – it has a hunting background and prefers wide open spaces. Houses with gardens are to be preferred. Height around 18 inches.*
EXERCISE NEEDS:	*Medium – a 20-minute run preferably twice a day.*
GROOMING NEEDS:	*High – 20 minutes' brushing per day.*
FOOD COSTS:	*Medium to low – three quarters of a pound of food a day.*

This is justifiably less popular than the larger Cavalier King Charles Spaniel because what it gains through compactness of size it loses in all-round versatility as a family pet. It is not as good a watchdog as a Cavalier, it is less happy being boarded with friends and it is more prone to eye problems because of its flattened face.

King Charles Spaniels can be a little snappy if teased by children, but they are generally very affectionate family pets, with intense loyalty to the people they live with. They will stand back from strangers until they are sure no harm will come.

They are more of a lap dog than Cavaliers, something that may endear them to the elderly living in compact homes.

DELINQUENCY RATING: *Low – can be awkward with the owner's friends.*
HOUSING NEEDS: *Low – suitable for small houses and flats. Around 12 inches in height.*
EXERCISE NEEDS: *Low –a good 10-minute run twice a day.*
GROOMING NEEDS: *Medium – 10 minutes a day.*
FOOD COSTS: *Low – half a pound of food a day.*

Choose the colour to match your decor, and the Labrador Retriever will give you excellent value for money as an all-round lovable family pet.

This is one of the most popular breeds in Britain today, mostly because of its lively, friendly temperament. It is extremely faithful and very tolerant of young children.

Occasionally some Labradors are a little too boisterous, and you may have to resort to Reform School techniques to bring them under control.

They are much less time-consuming than Golden Retrievers, partly because their exercise needs are lower, and partly because their coat is so smooth. Colours are black, yellow or chocolate.

DELINQUENCY RATING:	*Low – only the more boisterous ones need remedial training.*
HOUSING NEEDS:	*Medium to high – unsuitable for small houses or flats. Height 22 inches.*
EXERCISE NEEDS:	*Medium – a 20-minute run, preferably twice a day.*
GROOMING NEEDS:	*Low – five minutes' brushing daily.*
FOOD COSTS:	*Medium – one pound of food per day.*

Easily mistaken for the Fox Terrier, this is a comparatively new terrier breed, which avoids many of the faults of its near relatives. This is one of the best pet terriers around – lively, friendly and only rarely snappy.

The only real problem is its coat. Many Lakeland Terriers can hardly be seen for hair. They need regular clipping and about 20 minutes of brushing daily if they are to be kept looking their best.

Many Lakeland Terriers are shy with strangers, and are therefore not the best dogs for sociable families who want their pets to join in on every occasion. Having said that, they respond well to training and can be taught how to keep their distance until the family wants them near. There should be few problems in making the dog come when it's called, given good early training.

DELINQUENCY RATING:	*Low – be careful with strangers.*
HOUSING NEEDS:	*Low – smaller than the Fox Terrier. Suitable for small houses with small gardens. Height is 14 inches.*
EXERCISE NEEDS:	*Low – a 10-minute run, preferably twice a day.*
GROOMING NEEDS:	*High – 20 minutes' brushing daily.*
FOOD COSTS:	*Low – half to three quarters of a pound of food per day.*

A time-consuming dog, considering its size. Its grooming needs are high, and you may find yourself using the vacuum cleaner more than you would like.

Lhasas are affectionate, dependent lapdogs, most suited to single people who would like a loving companion, and are prepared to put in effort for this reward. It is not a good idea to have more than one dog, as they tend to fight. This is very difficult to train out, if not impossible. They have a very deep bark for such a small dog, but do not generally continue to make a noise for more than five minutes after a disturbance. For those with gardens, the dog is small enough to exercise itself – another plus point for the elderly.

DELINQUENCY RATING: *Low – neurotic if kennelled.*
HOUSING NEEDS: *Low – suited to the tiniest home. Height about 9 inches.*
EXERCISE NEEDS: *Low – a 10-minute walk every day.*
GROOMING NEEDS: *High – about 15 minutes of brushing a day.*
FOOD COSTS: *Low – about six ounces of food per day.*

This is really a ratting dog not a pet. It is very good at its job, but the qualities of seeking and destroying may make it a little difficult to live with around the home.

Manchester Terriers are often short-tempered, and occasionally snappy. You may have problems in the park because it may try to pick fights with smaller, and sometimes larger dogs.

With training, however, it is possible to suppress the dog's bad temper, and it will respond well to all the basic commands. It is not the most affectionate of dogs and cannot be recommended for families with small children.

On the plus side, grooming needs are minimal, and it will suit quite small homes. High-rise apartments may make it more snappy.

DELINQUENCY RATING: *High – may pick fights with other dogs.*
HOUSING NEEDS: *Medium – not suitable for high-rise apartments. Height about 15 inches.*
EXERCISE NEEDS: *Medium – a 20-minute run, preferably twice a day.*
GROOMING NEEDS: *Low – two or three minutes' brushing per day.*
FOOD COSTS: *Medium – one pound of food per day.*

People who have not got room for a Dobermann Pinscher often buy the miniature version for exactly the same reasons – their ability to get rid of unwanted strangers. This is a little dog with a big bark and a great deal of courage, which can become unwanted aggression in the wrong hands. It is a dog with a lot of nervous energy, which needs to be walked off every day. They don't usually start fights in the park because of their size. Their defence system is to issue a shrill shrieking whistle. But they can give a nasty bite if provoked.

They are as easy to train as Dobermanns, and are very clean animals around the house. They do not shed hair, and their short coat makes maintenance in wet weather trouble-free.

DELINQUENCY RATING:	*Medium – aggression is just below the surface.*
HOUSING NEEDS:	*Low – suitable for high-rise living; it stands at less than 12 inches tall.*
EXERCISE NEEDS:	*Medium – a high-energy dog, which likes a 20-minute run twice a day.*
GROOMING NEEDS:	*Low – no more than a couple of minutes a day.*
FOOD COSTS:	*Medium – a huge appetite for its size, one to one and a half pounds of food a day.*

As with the Standard Poodle, the breed's wool coat makes it very attractive to anyone who prefers a dog which does not shed hair. It will not mess up your carpets or furniture, and it will not affect people who are allergic to dog hair. This is an important quality in the Miniature and Toy varieties of poodle, since they have been bred to live indoors. You have to pay for this privilege – a visit to the hairdresser's every month will boost your running costs considerably.

Miniature poodles are very easy to train, and are extremely friendly. They respond well to children, and are very unlikely to be aggressive. You should have few problems with strangers who are invited into your home.

It is not necessary to have the dog shorn in the traditional lion-clip should you wish to cut down on grooming costs.

DELINQUENCY RATING:	*Low – friendly and obedient.*
HOUSING NEEDS:	*Medium to low – the ideal dog for the smaller house.*
EXERCISE NEEDS:	*Medium to low – a good 20-minute run once daily.*
GROOMING NEEDS:	*High – five to eight minutes of brushing per day, and clipping once every four to six weeks.*
FOOD COSTS:	*Medium to low – about one pound of food per day.*

You may have the usual delinquency problem of a breed designed as a shepherd dog: an uncontrollable urge to round up animals and people. But these are good all-round family dogs, well suited to life in the average semi. They are not the most outgoing of pets and may be shy when your friends visit your home. Some Miniature Schnauzers have a tendency to be nervous and may need encouragement to make them sociable.

With the family, however, they are capable of great affection, and their sturdy build makes them able to cope with most children's games.

Like most shepherding dogs, they respond well to obedience training, and you should have no problems making them come when they are called. Grooming is not arduous, but the beard must be kept clean.

DELINQUENCY RATING:	*Low – but watch for signs of nervousness in the puppy's parents.*
HOUSING NEEDS:	*Medium – a garden is preferred for extra exercise. Height is 12 to 14 inches.*
EXERCISE NEEDS:	*Medium – 20 minutes of running, preferably twice a day.*
GROOMING NEEDS:	*Medium to low – five to 10 minutes a day with special attention to the beard and eyebrows.*
FOOD COSTS:	*Low – eight ounces of food per day.*

You will have to be rich to afford the privilege of life with such a pet since it costs a small fortune to buy and to feed. It is a dog which loves water. In fact it has webbed feet, small folds of skin between its claws. In its native Canada it has been used as a water rescue dog for many years, pulling fully-grown men to shore in icy waters.

Its greasy top coat and soft undercoat, designed to keep it warm in low temperatures, can cause problems in centrally heated homes, especially when it moults.

These are probably the most placid dogs in the world and will adapt immediately to life in a stranger's home. They are the postman's favourite dog, but will protect the home against outright strangers.

DELINQUENCY RATING:	*Low – the best of temperaments.*
HOUSING NEEDS:	*High – they are massive, weighing in at between 110 and 140 pounds and standing 28 inches tall, but their placid nature makes a semi a possibility.*
EXERCISE NEEDS:	*High – a half-hour run (or swim) twice a day.*
GROOMING NEEDS:	*High – the long-coated variety has hair up to five inches long and needs at least 15 minutes' brushing every day.*
FOOD COSTS:	*High – between two and a half and five pounds of food a day depending on size.*

An Old English Sheepdog on a rainy day can carry an entire cloudful of water indoors. The effect can be devastating. It is the sheer size and length of coat of this dog which makes it such a handful. Grooming can take up to 20 minutes a day in wet weather, and it is vital to dry the dog thoroughly to prevent walls and furniture being soaked as the dog brushes against them.

These used to be cattle dogs, and occasionally their old aggressive instincts can come to the fore. Generally, however, it is their overpowering affection which necessitates early training. What seems amusing in a puppy can become a thorough nuisance when the dog leaps up at friends and strangers alike.

This is a dog best suited to a large house with a large garden, preferably near a park or open fields.

DELINQUENCY RATING: *High – adults weigh over 80 pounds and can easily knock children over or drag them into traffic.*

HOUSING NEEDS: *High – definitely not suitable for bedsitters. Houses with gardens only. Height 24 inches.*

EXERCISE NEEDS: *High – half an hour preferably twice a day in large open space.*

GROOMING NEEDS: *High – 10 to 15 minutes per day or the coat will tangle and leave deposits of hair around the house. Clipping every eight weeks.*

FOOD COSTS: *High – two pounds of food daily.*

This is a real show-off's pet, for someone who wants to look sophisticated and elegant like the king's courtesans of pre-Revolution France. The name is the French for butterfly and refers to the ears of the dog, which spread out like wings against the stark white "body" of the dog's face. But though it looks like a sad clown a Papillon is a very trainable dog – highly intelligent, the kind of animal that loves to perform tricks to gain attention.

They tend not to be snappy, and show considerable affection. You may have to be careful with small children since the dog is tiny and may feel the need to defend itself against teasing.

Grooming is comparatively time-consuming for such a small dog because of the magnificent feathering on the tail, legs, chest and neck.

DELINQUENCY RATING:	*Low – unless teased.*
HOUSING NEEDS:	*Low – it may be 12 inches tall but it is only about four pounds in weight and will fit easily into a high-rise flat.*
EXERCISE NEEDS:	*Low – a 10-minute walk every day.*
GROOMING NEEDS:	*High – 15 minutes' brushing per day.*
FOOD COSTS:	*Low – a quarter to half a pound of food per day.*

This is a high-status dog for people with small amounts of space. Pekes have a reputation for bad temper, which probably owes more to their tetchy owners than the dog itself. They respond well to training, and can be kept out of trouble quite easily by the owner picking them up and holding them out of harm's way.

The biggest problem with Pekes is their coats. They need to be combed very lightly using bristle brushes to avoid spoiling their fringe hair. In centrally heated houses they will moult very heavily in Spring and Winter. The initial cost can be relatively high, but thereafter their needs are small. They make ideal pets for the elderly because they need little exercise, and are quite easy to train.

DELINQUENCY RATING:	*Low – any bad temper is easy to suppress.*
HOUSING NEEDS:	*Low – suitable for high-rise apartments. Height six to 10 inches.*
EXERCISE NEEDS:	*Low – a 10-minute run every day.*
GROOMING NEEDS:	*High – 10 to 15 minutes daily, taking care not to damage the fringes on the legs, chest and neck.*
FOOD COSTS:	*Low – a quarter-pound of finely minced meat and biscuit a day.*

A good-natured miniature spitz breed, which makes an ideal pet for anyone on a small income, with limited accommodation. Unlike many small terriers this breed tends to have a friendly disposition with little tendency to snap.

It takes a lot of grooming time for its size because its coat looks best when it is frothed up all over. Failure to put in a good quarter of an hour's brushing every day will result in a great many shed hairs, which in the brightly coloured varieties can mess up furniture and clothes. The dog adapts well to families with small children, but there may be a tendency to think it is sturdier than it is. Its coat conceals a very light-framed body, which can easily be hurt by young children.

They are intelligent dogs, which respond very quickly to training, and make ideal pets for the elderly because their exercise needs are so low.

DELINQUENCY RATING: Low – but warn children to handle the dog carefully.
HOUSING NEEDS: Low – it weighs in at only five pounds and is only 11 inches tall. Suitable for the smallest home.
EXERCISE NEEDS: Low – a 10-minute walk per day.
GROOMING NEEDS: High – 15 minutes' brushing per day.
FOOD COSTS: Low – a quarter- to a half-pound of food a day.

This tiny dog may look tough, but it has more in common with a Pekingese than a Bulldog. It was bred as a lapdog, and has taken well to life in the concrete jungle.

But there are problems. Because they are so short-haired, they do not acclimatise well to extremes of heat or cold. You may have to wrap them in a coat in winter and keep them out of the sun in summer. Pugs have been known to suffocate easily in cars left out in the sun. Their flat faces restrict their breathing in such circumstances.

They can be self-willed, and need firm training. But they are not aggressive, they do not bark a great deal, and are good watch-dogs.

They need their faces wiping daily to prevent the build-up of bacteria in the wrinkles around the forehead and eyes.

DELINQUENCY RATING: *Low – but be firm in training.*
HOUSING NEEDS: *Low – ideal for small-scale living. Height about 12 inches.*
EXERCISE NEEDS: *Low – a 10-minute run, preferably twice a day.*
GROOMING NEEDS: *Low – the short coat needs brushing only once a week for between five and 10 minutes. The face needs wiping daily with damp cotton wool.*
FOOD COSTS: *Low – six to seven ounces of food per day.*

If you can afford a big dog, this is just about the best choice in terms of temperament. It is huge – around 30 inches tall and weighing about a hundred pounds – but it is gentle, kind and surprisingly at home indoors. Pyreneans are considerably less bulky than Newfoundlands, and their food needs are proportionately smaller. They have a gait like a drunken sailor, which may cause accidents around the home, so remember to keep ornaments out of their way.

They are very good guard-dogs, repelling intruders by their size and depth of voice, but they are easy to control, since aggression is not high. They are very tolerant of young children. Grooming needs are less than for a Newfoundland, but because of their light-coloured coats you may have to make considerable efforts in wet weather. Shampooing a dog of this size takes a long time.

DELINQUENCY RATING:	*Low – a gentle giant.*
HOUSING NEEDS:	*High – you need lots of space and a fairly large garden.*
EXERCISE NEEDS:	*High – a 30-minute run twice daily.*
GROOMING NEEDS:	*High – 20 minutes' brushing daily, and regular shampooing.*
FOOD COSTS:	*High – two and a half pounds of food a day.*

Another big, powerful and friendly dog. This is everyone's idea of how a favourite uncle should be. Its reputation as a rescue dog in the Alpine passes is justly earned. The advent of modern rescue techniques has confined it to the home, where its size makes it look very much out of place. But its genuine affection for the family overcomes any problems if the home is big enough.

St Bernards are very unaggressive, but make good guard-dogs because of their loyalty and their desire to defend the home. They like playing with small children, and because they respond well to training, they should present few behaviour problems.

The rough-haired variety creates grooming problems for those with limited time. You have the choice of the smooth-haired dog to cut down the amount of brushing needed every day.

DELINQUENCY RATING: *Low – big and soft with no aggression.*
HOUSING NEEDS: *High – only suitable for larger homes with larger gardens. Height about 30 inches.*
EXERCISE NEEDS: *High – a 30-minute walk twice a day.*
GROOMING NEEDS: *High – 20 minutes' brushing a day for the rough-haired variety, 10 minutes daily for the smooth-haired.*
FOOD COSTS: *High – two pounds of food per day.*

This is really an Arctic pack dog and can cause a great deal of aggro when kept as a pet. It is wilful and may well fight with other dogs in the park, and take a bite at strangers who venture too close to its territory. Its biggest problem is its long thick coat, especially during its twice-yearly moult. Because it is bred for survival in cold climates it sheds hair a great deal in centrally heated rooms. Some owners have saved the combings of the undercoat to spin into knitting yarn.

This is not a dog for small houses because it needs a large garden in which to let off steam. You must show it who is boss at an early age, or obedience could be a real problem. If you have mastered the dog, it can prove very loving and friendly and adapts well to small children.

DELINQUENCY RATING: *High – often disobedient and aggressive.*
HOUSING NEEDS: *High – a large dog, which would prefer a country home with a large garden. Height is about 21 inches.*
EXERCISE NEEDS: *High – a 30-minute run twice a day.*
GROOMING NEEDS: *High – 15 to 20 minutes' brushing every day to avoid tangling and annoying hair loss.*
FOOD COSTS: *Medium – a pound of food a day.*

Not as good a choice as a West Highland White Terrier because it can be stubborn and aggressive. This is a dog with a strong temperament which will not behave itself to order. It has got to be mastered to get any degree of obedience.

Once the hard work is over, the Scottie can be a pleasing house dog, suited to life in high-rise flats.

It is a low-slung dog and you will have problems on rainy days – it can pick up large quantities of dirt and will smell unless dried immediately with a good rough towel.

Some Scotties can be aggressive not only with other dogs but with visitors to the home. Prevention is always the best course.

DELINQUENCY RATING:	*Medium – a streak of real Celtic fire.*
HOUSING NEEDS:	*Low – suitable for bedsit living. Height 10 to 11 inches.*
EXERCISE NEEDS:	*Low – a 10-minute run twice a day.*
GROOMING NEEDS:	*Low to medium – a coarse coat which needs five to 10 minutes of vigorous brushing daily.*
FOOD COSTS:	*Low – half to one pound of food per day.*

All the appeal of a Rough Collie but only two thirds the size. This is an intelligent, friendly dog, which makes the perfect pet for modest family homes.

Shelties have been very successful in obedience competitions, a reflection of their sheepdog background in the Shetland Isles. You should have few problems in getting the dog to understand and obey.

They make good watch-dogs, staying alert for any intruder, and barking loudly to warn them off. Unlike many hounds, continued barking should not be a problem.

Most of the time they are quiet dogs, very friendly with young children, and undemanding in terms of exercise. This makes them a good choice for busy parents.

Grooming needs are high but far less than for the Rough Collie because of its size.

DELINQUENCY RATING:	*Low – very difficult to provoke.*
HOUSING NEEDS:	*Low – a small house is better than a high-rise apartment. Height 14 inches.*
EXERCISE NEEDS:	*Medium to low – a 20-minute run daily.*
GROOMING NEEDS:	*High – 10 to 15 minutes' brushing daily.*
FOOD COSTS:	*Low to medium – three quarters to a pound of food per day.*

A more outgoing breed than the Pekingese, its main problem is the time needed for grooming. It has so much hair that many owners groom it thoroughly by instalments – one leg a night. Owners must be gentle so as not to damage the coat and special attention must be paid to eyes and ears.

This is a very loving dog, and is generally quite strong enough to take rough play with children. Occasionally inbreeding will create a snappy dog, and care must be taken to look at the parents of any puppy you intend to buy.

It is a dog suitable for life in a flat, and after the initial buying cost should not prove expensive to run. Fights with other dogs are unlikely but it may be unwise to own more than one of its breed as they may fight amongst themselves.

DELINQUENCY RATING: *Low – a generally placid dog.*
HOUSING NEEDS: *Medium to low – prefers a small garden. Height 11 inches.*
EXERCISE NEEDS: *Medium to low – a 20-minute run, preferably twice a day.*
GROOMING NEEDS: *High – 10 to 15 minutes' gentle brushing every day.*
FOOD COSTS: *Low – half a pound of food a day.*

Skye Terriers have a reputation for biting. But the breed has quietened down in the last 20 years, and seems less likely to have a go at humans than other small dogs.

They have been used successfully as badger dogs in recent years, going to ground in packs. They are brave and tenacious.

In the home they are generally friendly and happy dogs, but they are very cautious of strangers. They will bark loud and long whenever a stranger approaches the house, and may be difficult to keep quiet.

Their long coat is quite easy to groom, and there is little problem with hairs on furniture and clothes.

When they play with children they will let it be known when they have had enough, usually by growling. Be careful not to let things go too far.

DELINQUENCY RATING: *Medium – will bite if provoked.*
HOUSING NEEDS: *Medium – quite a heavy dog despite its small height of 10 inches. Needs a small garden.*
EXERCISE NEEDS: *Medium – 20-minute run, preferably twice a day.*
GROOMING NEEDS: *Low – five minutes' brushing a day, and a thorough grooming every two weeks.*
FOOD COSTS: *Low – eight to nine ounces of food per day.*

A real Jekyll and Hyde dog. It is a ferocious fighter with other dogs, yet all sweetness and light with human beings.

Staffordshire Bull Terriers must be kept out of fights at all costs when young. Their owners must simply avoid contact with other dogs in these formative years, or their pet will develop an insatiable taste for a fight.

A home with a garden is essential so that the dog can exercise without meeting the temptation of other fighting dogs. If the owners are unlucky and a fight starts they can usually drag the dog out of trouble by squeezing its collar.

Surprisingly they are friendly and placid in the home and will stand any amount of rough and tumble with young children, without thinking of biting. They rarely bark, but will quietly let you know if intruders are near.

DELINQUENCY RATING: *High – the dog to start a fight.*
HOUSING NEEDS: *High – garden vital for trouble-free exercise even though the dog is only 15 inches tall.*
EXERCISE NEEDS: *Medium – a 20-minute run twice a day.*
GROOMING NEEDS: *Low – five minutes' brushing every day.*
FOOD COSTS: *Low – ten ounces per day for the adult, a pound a day for the growing youngster.*

If you are house-proud, and want a medium-sized all-round family pet, the Standard Poodle is the dog for you. Unlike most dogs, poodles grow wool rather than hair. For this reason, they do not shed their coats, and are particularly valued in households where one member of the family has an allergy to dog hair, the kind that brings on attacks of asthma. They are very intelligent, exceptionally sociable animals which respond very well to training.

The only disadvantage is that they require considerable grooming every day to stop their wool tangling, and regular monthly visits to the salon. This will add to your running costs considerably. Otherwise, poodles are excellent value and should rate very highly on anyone's shortlist for a non-delinquent dog.

DELINQUENCY RATING: *Low – very friendly and obedient.*
HOUSING NEEDS: *Medium – if you want a poodle for a high-rise apartment, choose a Toy Poodle. Standard Poodles are around 15 to 22 inches tall.*
EXERCISE NEEDS: *Medium – a 20-minute run preferably twice a day.*
GROOMING NEEDS: *High – needs eight to 10 minutes' brushing a day, and clipping every month to six weeks.*
FOOD COSTS: *Medium – about one and a half pounds of food daily.*

Like the German Shepherd Dog, the Tervueren and its close relative the Groenendael have all been used for police work. This is a large, powerful dog, which is extremely responsive to training. It is said by some to have a less aggressive temperament than the German Shepherd Dog, but in irresponsible hands it could prove a problem if it is not properly trained. It will be very defensive of the household, keeping strangers at bay.

Its long coat needs about 15 minutes' brushing every day to prevent matting, a factor which gives the smooth-coated German Shepherd Dog an advantage. It is cheaper to feed, however, and this may prove the deciding factor for families on modest incomes.

DELINQUENCY RATING: *Medium – it is a large dog, which could do a lot of damage if badly trained.*
HOUSING NEEDS: *High – medium to large houses only. Height is 22 to 26 inches.*
EXERCISE NEEDS: *High – a half-hour run morning and evening.*
GROOMING NEEDS: *High – 15 minutes' brushing daily.*
FOOD COSTS: *Medium – about one and a quarter pounds of food per day.*

Many people see Toy Poodles as nothing but rich women's lapdogs. Clipped in the traditional manner, they look the ultimate in decorative dogs. But beneath the fur, they are very intelligent, friendly and obedient pets ideally suited to anyone with limited accommodation or time.

These are very small dogs – under 10 inches in height – and are therefore suitable for people living in high-rise accommodation where the dog may have to be confined for much of the day. Their exercise needs are low. A good 10-minute run once a day will be enough for most pets – but try to give them much longer runs at weekends.

Grooming needs are considerably less than for the Miniature or Standard Poodle, but you will need to visit the hairdresser's just as often – at much the same cost.

DELINQUENCY RATING: *Low – friendly and quick to learn.*
HOUSING NEEDS: *Low – one of the dogs best suited to high-rise apartments. Height is 10 inches or less.*
EXERCISE NEEDS: *Low – 10 minutes once a day.*
GROOMING NEEDS: *High – five minutes of brushing per day and clipping every four to six weeks.*
FOOD COSTS: *Low – about eight ounces of food per day.*

For a terrier this is quite a cheerful little chap. It has all the stubbornness and fearlessness of its breed, but is much happier in disposition than most terriers. It therefore makes a very good house pet even for those in high-rise homes.

Its pure white colour may cause you problems in wet weather, but luckily, it is not as low-slung as its near cousin the Scottish Terrier. It would be wise to have a supply of old towels set aside for the dog on wet days. Westies are quick to learn, and respond well to praise. Some may be a little snappy with other dogs, but their size makes them easy to control.

They are good with children, but will not want to play for too long. They make ideal pets for the elderly because of their size and low exercise needs.

DELINQUENCY RATING:	*Medium to low – an unterrier-like nice streak.*
HOUSING NEEDS:	*Low – well suited to high-rise living. Height about 11 inches.*
EXERCISE NEEDS:	*Low – a 10-minute walk twice a day.*
GROOMING NEEDS:	*Medium – about 10 to 15 minutes' brushing per day; regular shampooing in wet weather.*
FOOD COSTS:	*Low – a quarter to half a pound of food per day.*

Like the Greyhound, this is a dog designed for one job — chasing game. Its modern equivalent is a racing animal, and if kept as a pet should almost be treated as if you intend to enter it for the local Whippet derby. Otherwise the dog may become neurotic.

A Whippet intends to kill when it sets off after the hare, and this aggressive instinct may cause a few problems with small dogs in the park. Strict obedience training must be started early, concentrating on getting the dog to come when it is called. Unless this is mastered, you may have to wait a very long time for your dog to tire of a run in open country. They are not the most affectionate of pets at home, but with good exercise they may enjoy company. They may not tolerate young children.

DELINQUENCY RATING:	Medium — not a fighter, more a chaser.
HOUSING NEEDS:	Medium — very much smaller than the Greyhound at 18 inches tall. Garden not essential.
EXERCISE NEEDS:	High — a good 30-minute run twice a day.
GROOMING NEEDS:	Low — three to four minutes daily.
FOOD COSTS:	Medium — a pound of food a day.

This is a dog tailor-made for high-rise apartments and people on a small income. It is so tiny that it can get nearly all the exercise it needs by running around the house – a quality which makes it a good buy for the elderly. It is a terrier, with the potential for a hot temper, but at only five to six inches in height, and weighing only seven to nine pounds, it is very easy to keep in order.

Yorkies do need a fair amount of grooming to keep their feathery coats in good condition. They may need drying off with a towel when you have taken them for a walk in wet weather, but this will not take long.

They are responsive to training, but you must be gentle with a check-chain to prevent yourself harming them. They are very easy to control on a lead, and if they get into trouble with other dogs, you can always pick them up and put them under your arm. This is, again, very useful for the elderly who might feel nervous about controlling a larger dog.

DELINQUENCY RATING:	*Low – most have lively, friendly temperaments.*
HOUSING NEEDS:	*Low – quite at home in high-rise flats.*
EXERCISE NEEDS:	*Low – 10 minutes a day if you can find time.*
GROOMING NEEDS:	*Medium – eight to 10 minutes' brushing every day.*
FOOD COSTS:	*Low – a quarter-pound of food per day.*